FORTIFIED CITIES OF ANCIENT INDIA

Cultural, Historical and Textual Studies of South Asian Religions

The volumes featured in the Anthem **Cultural, Historical and Textual Studies of South Asian Religions** series are the expression of an international community of scholars committed to the reshaping of the field of textual and historical studies of religions. Titles in this series examine practice, ritual, and other textual religious products, crossing different area studies and time frames. Featuring a vast range of interpretive perspectives, this innovative series aims to enhance the way we look at religious traditions.

FORTIFIED CITIES OF ANCIENT INDIA

A COMPARATIVE STUDY

Dieter Schlingloff

ANTHEM PRESS
LONDON · NEW YORK · DELHI

Anthem Press
An imprint of Wimbledon Publishing Company
www.anthempress.com

This edition first published in UK and USA 2014
by ANTHEM PRESS
75–76 Blackfriars Road, London SE1 8HA, UK
or PO Box 9779, London SW19 7ZG, UK
and
244 Madison Ave. #116, New York, NY 10016, USA

First published in hardback by Anthem Press in 2013

Layout by Marianna Ferrara

Cover image courtesy of Dominik Oczkowski

British Library Cataloguing in Publication Data
A catalogue record for this book is available from the British Library.

Library of Congress Cataloging in Publication Data
A catalog record for this book has been requested.

ISBN-13: 978 1 78308 349 7 (Pbk)
ISBN-10: 1 78308 349 2 (Pbk)

This title is also available as an ebook.

Dedicated to the memory of Herbert Härtel (1921-2005),
the excavator of Sonkh (Mathura)

Plan of a city gate excavated in Sisupalgarh with its details as prescribed in *Kauṭilīya Arthaśāstra 2.3.17-28* (p. 76-78)

tribhāga-godhāmukhaṃ gopuraṃ (*KA 2.3.31*, p. 81)

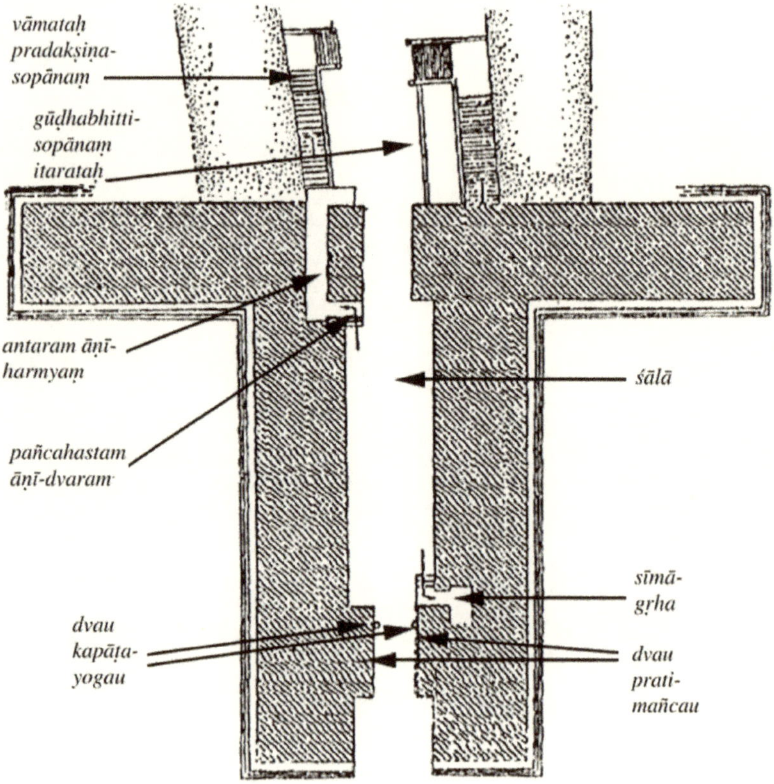

Conjectural reconstruction based on the prescriptions in *Kauṭilīya Arthaśāstra 2.3.6-8, 31* (p. 61-62)

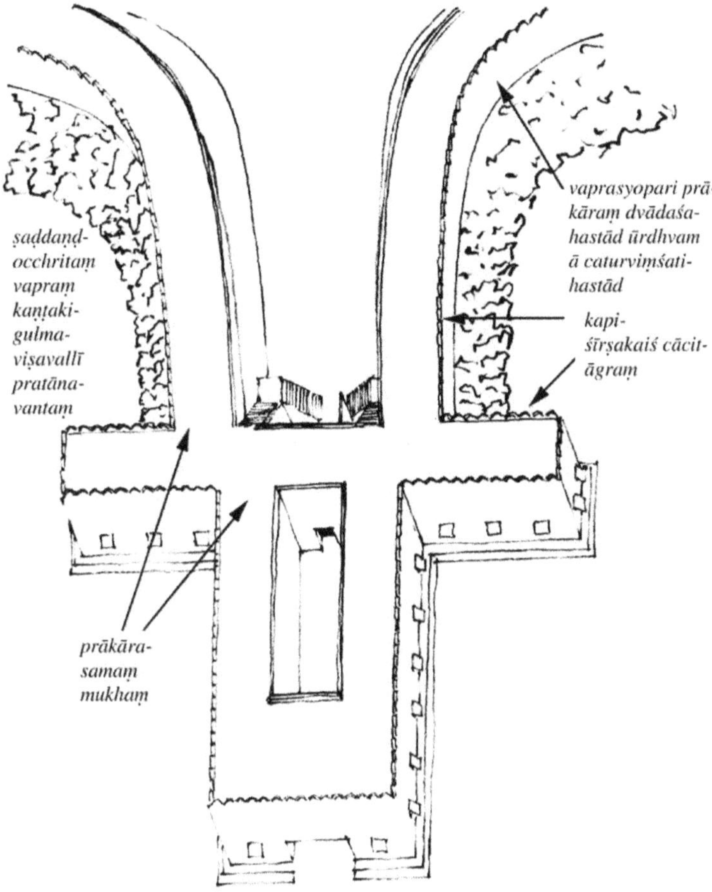

Acknowledgments

Translation from the German by Paul Yule. Revisions and editing by Patrick Olivelle, assisted by Oliver Freiberger. Drawings by Waldtraut Schlingloff (†) (Chs. 1 and 2) and Monika Zin (Ch. 3). Gate reconstruction by Dominik Oczkowski. Formatting by Monika Zin.

Summary of Contents

Chapter 1. The Layout of the City 11

The analysis of the reference to towns in epic, Buddhist and Jain literature shows that such texts contain a variety of stock phrases concerning city architecture (p. 11-14). Specialist statements contained in the Kauṭilīya Arthaśāstra elucidate these (p. 14-16). A survey of the results of archaeological research (p. 16-28) verifies these statements and confirms the planning of Old Indian cities (p. 28-29). The investigation of house architecture (p. 30-32) illuminates the question of the population density in the cities, which had the same dimension as contemporary Greek and Roman cities (p. 32). According to Megasthenes, Pāṭaliputra, however, was 10-20 times larger than the usual towns; nearly double the size of imperial Rome, it was the greatest city of the ancient world (p. 32-33). Combining the notes of Megasthenes with statements from Indian literature (p. 33-35) and archaeology (p. 35-37), the boundaries of ancient Pāṭaliputra can be reconstructed (p. 37-40). This proves that the Bhikna Pahadi was on the one hand, in accordance with the prescriptions of the Kauṭilīya, a monument in the center of the city (p. 39-40); Kumrahar, on the other, never could have been a palatial area, but rather was a pleasure hall outside the city wall (p. 40-43). After investigating the historical development of Pāṭaliputra (p. 43-46), the similarities and differences in the development of Greek and Indian cities are discussed which proves that the different constitutions of the states are conform with the different positions of Greek and Indian cityscapes (p. 46-48). Overview (p. 49). Figures 1-29 (p. 52-56).

Chapter 2. The Construction of a Fortification 57

The chapter on city fortifications in the Arthaśāstra, regarded as the most obscure in Kauṭilya's work, is elucidated by the results of excavations as as by building technical and military considerations (p. 57-59). Its prescriptions regarding the size and form of moats, ramparts and walls (p. 59-63) generally correspond with the archaeological finds (p. 63-69). The texts continues with the description of the defenses, viz. towers, embrasures etc. (p. 69-72). The most elaborate description concerns the city gates, details of which reveal a striking similarity with gates, especially in Sisupalgarh and Śrāvastī (p. 72-82). Lexicographical results (p. 83-84). Figures 1-30 (p. 86-90).

Chapter 3. The Model of the City in Narrative Ajanta Paintings 91

Some of the narrative Ajanta paintings show the depicted events embedded into an ideal city plan. This plan, divested of the figures acting in them reveals a generalized sketch of the cityscape which may complete the picture of the cities of Ancient India elaborated on in chapters 1 and 2 (p. 91-92). Figures 1-8 (p. 93-96).

List of Abbreviations 97

Index 101

About the Author 111

Chapter 1

*The Layout of the City**

The oldest literary documents of the Indo-Arians, namely the Vedas, communicate to us the image of a rural way of life.[1] An entirely different way of life is revealed by the oldest texts of the Buddhists and Jainas, as also by the great epics: they occur before a background of an urban culture. Flourishing cities form the centers of mighty states. The life of the city-dwellers is illuminated from all sides, while that of rural settlements and their inhabitants decline into obscure ahistoricity.

Strewn among their tales, sagas and legends are numerous descriptions of cities. Thus, Ayodhyā, the residence of the epic hero Rāma, is portrayed in the Rāmāyaṇa in the following manner:

> (7) 12 miles long and 3 miles wide is the great and splendid city. It has well-laid-out main streets (8) and is graced with a large and well-laid-out royal highway that is bestrewn with fallen flowers and continuously sprinkled with water. (9) King Daśaratha ... lived in this city —(10) it had gates with door-panels, well-laid-out interior shops, and all sorts of war machines and weapons; in it lived all kinds of craftsmen; (11) crowded with heralds and bards. it was splendid and of unequalled grandeur, with high towers and flags and filled with hundreds of "hundred-killer" weapons; (12) it was a city graced everywhere with throngs of women and dancers, containing parks and mango groves, a vast city girded by sal-trees;

* Revised and enlarged translation from the German *Die altindische Stadt. Eine vergleichende Untersuchung.* Wiesbaden 1969.

[1] Cf. W. Rau, *Staat und Gesellschaft im alten Indien, nach den Brāhmaṇa-Texten dargestellt,* Wiesbaden 1957, p. 51ff.; also p. 126 (transl.): "Vedic antiquity knew settlements which by no means earn" (the name city), and note 6: "The word *nagara* = city, appears first in the latest layers of our texts."

(13) it was a fort with an inaccessible and deep moat, unconquerable by foreigners, and filled with horses and elephants, as well as with cattle, camels and donkeys; (14) it was packed with throngs of vassal kings bringing tributes and graced with traders from diverse regions; (15) it was adorned with palaces decorated with jewels resembling mountains; it was brimming with pavilions and resembled the heavenly city of the King of gods.[2]

The following account of the residence of King Milinda occurs in the Buddhist didactic narrative *Milindapañha*:

...the city Sāgala,[3] which lies in a lovely area graced with rivers and mountains, with groves, parks, woods, lakes and lotus ponds, winsome in the midst of rivers, mountains and forests; built by able men, not pressured by adversaries and enemies who have been subdued; with manifold different towers and tower-gates; with a castle containing excellent gates and gate arches and surrounded by a deep moat and a light plastered fortification wall; with well-laid streets, intersections, crossings and triangular places; with interior shops which are filled with numerous excellent, well-decorated wares; enhanced with hundreds of different alms houses, with hundred thousands of wonderful dwellings that resemble the mountain peeks of the Himalayas; decorated; ...[a description follows of the city dwellers]...; furnished with different textile shops containing Kāśika, Kautumbaraka etc. (cloth); scented by fragrance of the perfume shops with well-decorated splendid manifold flowers; filled with many wonderful gemstones; enlivened by stately merchants with well-decorated shops visible from all sides; filled with coins, silver, gold, copper and pottery; a site of glowing treasures, rich in money, corn, luxury goods and utensils; filled with treasure and storage houses, and with great amounts of food and drink — many kinds of food and drink for munching, eating, licking, drinking and tasting; appearing like Uttarakuru, filled with corn, like Alakamanda, the city of gods.[4]

[2] Rām. 1,5,7ff.: *āyatā daśa ca dve ca yojanāni mahāpurī śrīmatī trīṇi vistīrṇā suvibhakta-mahāpathā* ||*7*|| *rājamārgeṇa mahatā suvibhaktena śobhitā mukta-puṣpāvakīrṇena jala-siktena nityaśaḥ* ||*8*|| *tāṃ tu rājā Daśaratho ... purīm āvāsayām āsa* ... ||*9*|| *kapāṭa-toraṇavatīṃ suvibhaktāntarāpaṇām sarva-yantrāyudhavatīm uṣitāṃ sarva-śilpibhiḥ* ||*10*|| *sūta-māgadha-saṃbādhāṃ śrīmatīm atula-prabhām uccāṭṭāla-dhvajavatīṃ śataghnī-śata-saṃkulām* ||*11*|| *vadhū-nāṭaka-saṅghaiś ca saṃyuktāṃ sarvataḥ purīm udyānāmravaṇopetāṃ mahatīṃ sāla-mekhalām* ||*12*|| *durga-gambhīra-parikhāṃ durgām anyair durāsadām vāji-vāraṇa-sampūrṇāṃ gobhir uṣṭraiḥ kharais tathā* ||*13*|| *sāmanta-rāja-saṃghaiś ca bali-karmabhir āvṛtām nānā-deśa-nivāsaiś ca vaṇigbhir upaśobhitām* | |*14*|| *prāsādai ratna-vikṛtaiḥ parvatair iva śobhitām kūṭāgārais ca saṃpūrṇām Indrasyev Āmaravatīm* ||*15*||.

[3] = Skt. *śākala;* in the epic, capital of the Madra country. Ptolemy VII, p. 46 also mentions the city Sāgala; according to Fleet it is identical with the modern Sialkot in the Panjab.

[4] Mil. 1-2: ... *Sāgalan nāma nagaraṃ nadī-pabbata-sobhitaṃ ramanīya-bhūmi ppadesa-bhāgaṃ ārāmuyyānôpavana-taḷāka-pokkharaṇī-sampannaṃ nadī-pabbata-*

A stereotypical description of a city in the Jaina canon reads as follows:

> ... the city (so-and-so), rich, safe, and wealthy; ... (followed by a characterization of the land and its inhabitants) ... ; provided with precious groves, parks, springs, ponds, bathing pools, and wells; with a widely protruding and deeply dug moat, surrounded by an arched fortification wall that is thick and hard to conquer, due to its double-wing gates and discuses, maces, cudgels, barriers and hundred-killers; boasting arched battlements; high looming with its towers, pathways, gates, gate buildings, and gate arches; with a well-built royal street; with firm crossbars and door posts fashioned by enabled masters; contentedly and happily filled with craftsmen who enliven markets and bazaars; adorned with shops of manifold treasures at triangular places, street forks, intersections, and crossways; ...(followed by the description of street life)...; provided with lightly plastered, exquisite residential houses; a feast for the eyes, uplifting and worth seeing, shapely and perfect in form.[5]

Although these three texts derive from different languages (the first in epic Sanskrit,[6] the second in Pāli[7] and the third in

vanarāmaṇeyyakaṃ sutavanta-nimmitaṃ nihata-paccatthika-paccāmittaṃ anupapīḷitaṃ vividha-vicitra-daḷham ṭṭāla-koṭṭakaṃ vara-pavara-gopura-toraṇaṃ gambhīr-parikhā-paṇḍara-pākāra-parikkhitt-antepuraṃ suvibhatta-vīthi-caccara-catukka-singhāṭakaṃ suppasāritānekavidha-vara-bhaṇḍa-paripūrit-antarāpaṇaṃ vividha-dānagga- satasamupa-sobhitaṃ himagiri-sikhara-sankāsa-vara-bhavana-satasahassa-patimaṇḍitaṃ ... kāsika-koṭumbarakādi-nānāvidha-vatthāpaṇa-sampannaṃ suppasārita-rucira-bahuvidha puppha-gandhāpaṇa-gandha-gandhitaṃ āsiṃsaniya-bahu-ratana-paripūritaṃ disāmukha-suppasāritāpaṇasingāra-vāṇija-gaṇānucaritaṃ kahāpaṇa-rajata-suvaṇṇa-kaṃsapatthara-paripūraṃ pajjotamāna-nidhi-niketaṃ pahūta-dhana-dhañña-vittūpakaraṇaṃ paripuṇṇa-kosa-koṭṭhāgāraṃ bahv annapānaṃ bahuvidha-khajja-bhojja-leyya-peyya-sāyaniyaṃ Uttarakuru-sankāsaṃ sampanna-sassaṃ Āḷakamandā viya devapurāṃ.

[5] ... (*Campā nāma*) *nayarī ... riddha-tthimiya-samiddhā ... ārām-ujjāṇa-agaḍa-talaga-dīhiya-vappiṇa-guṇovaveyā uvviddha-viula-gambhīra-khāta-phalihā cakka-gaya-musuṇḍhi-oroha-sayagghi-jamala-kavāḍa-ghaṇa-duppavesā dhaṇu-kuḍila-vanka-pāgāra-parikkhittā kavisīsaga-vaṭṭa-raiya-saṃṭhiya-virāyamāṇā aṭṭālaya-cariya-dāra-gopura-toraṇa-unnayā suvibhatta-rāya-maggā chey 'āyariya-raiya-daḍha-phaliha-indakhīlā vivaṇi-vaṇi-cchitta-sippiyāiṇṇa-nivvuya-suhā singhāḍaga-tiga-caukka-caccara-paṇiy 'āvaṇa-viviha-vasu-parimaṇḍiyā ... paṇḍura-vara-bhavaṇa-sanni-mahiyā uttāṇa-nayaṇa-pecchaṇijjā pāsādīyā darisaṇijjā abhirūvā paḍirūvā;* quoted in E. Leumann, *Das Aupapātika Sūtra, erstes Upāṅga der Jaina*, Leipzig 1883, p. 21.

[6] The descriptions of cities in the two epics Mahābhārata and Rāmāyaṇa are treated in a monograph by J.K. de Cock, *Eene oudindische stad volgens het Epos*, Diss. Phil. Amsterdam 1899.

[7] The terms regarding the cityscape of the Buddhist Pāli canon are treated by K.T.S. Sarao, see Ch. 2, note 1. On the shortcomings of the study by A.K. Coomaraswamy, *Early Indian Architecture I. Cities and City-Gates* (EA II, 1930, p. 213ff.), see Ch. 2, p. 58, note 1.

Jaina Prakrit[8]), the correspondences are obvious. Notwithstanding the eulogies, the descriptions consist of certain basic ideas: the cities possess well-laid-out[9] streets[10], intersections, and places[11] with all kinds of shops;[12] they are defended by ramparts[13] and walls with towers[14] and gates[15], as well as by a deep moat.[16] Lastly, they are surrounded by parks.[17] The nomenclature freezes to fixed phrases, which in all three language areas recur in numerous passages without ever being explained. The narrators' intention was not to make such explanations, but rather to decorate the generally known concepts with especially well-sounding decorative words.

Nevertheless, the fact that already in the pre-Christian era written works on city building existed can be determined from later texts. Discussions regarding urban complexes occur as well in Indian medieval books on architecture, as also in the Kauṭilīya Arthaśāstra, a compendium on statecraft allegedly written by the prime minister of the Maurya ruler Candragupta, around 300 BCE in Pāṭaliputra. A comparison of the relevant passages[18] reveals that

[8] Architectural terms of the Jaina canon are dealt with by Moti Chandra, *Architectural Data in Jain Canonical Literature,* JBBRAS, NS 26, 1951, p. 169ff.

[9] *suvibhakta,* below, Ch. 1, note 73.

[10] Apparently without differentiation, the designations *rathyā* and *vīthī* are used for street. A main artery is called *mahā-rathyā* or *mahā-patha,* and a side street *upa-rathyā.* When dealing with a market street, one speaks of *āpaṇa-rathyā* or *āpaṇa-vīthī.* The "royal street" is a main street that leads straight from the gate to the castle: *rāja-mārga, rāja-patha, rāja-vīthī.*

[11] A stereotypical list of different kinds of places is available in the Pāli canon (see above, Ch. 1, note 4: *...caccara-catukka-singhāṭakaṃ)* and in the Jaina canon (above, Ch. 1, note 5: *singhāḍaga-tiga-caukka-caccara-paṇiy 'āvaṇa...);* in the Jaina canon also from the Kalpasūtra (ed. W. Schubring, Diss. Straßburg 1905, 1, 12): *āvaṇa-gihaṃsi vā racchā-muhaṃsi vā siṅghaḍaṃsi vā tiyaṃsi vā caukkaṃsi vā caccaraṃsi vā antarāvaṇaṃsi vā* "in a house with a shop, on the main street, on triangular places, street forks, intersections, crossways, or in indoor shops".

[12] The distinction between *āpaṇa* ("shop") and *antarāpaṇa* ("interior shop") remains unclear. Both are located on the main streets. Perhaps in the first case we are dealing with open stands, and in the other, with shops in the interior of dwellings. The commentary on the above-mentioned Kalpasūtra explains an interior shop as "a house which itself is a shop" (2301: *yad vā gṛham svayam evāpaṇas tad antarāpaṇaḥ). vipaṇi* seems, on the other hand, to refer to "market", "bazaar".

[13] The rampart is designated as *vapra* or *caya,* the wall as *prākāra.* For *sāla, śāla* with the meaning "wall", see below, p. 45 note 156, and Ch. 2, note 22.

[14] *aṭṭa, aṭṭāla;* see below, Ch. 2, notes 48f.

[15] *dvāra, gopura, pratolī;* cf. Ch. 2, p. 81f.

[16] City moats *(parikhā)* are as wide as the ocean (Mbh. 1,199,29) and filled with fish and crocodiles (Mbh. 3,268,3; 12,69,41).

[17] *udyāna,* "park", *ārama,* "grove", *vana,* "forest", *upavana,* "woods", *pramādavana,* "pleasure forest". The designations for different kinds of bathing ponds include *taḍāga, hrada, vāpī, dīrghikā, nalinī, puṣkariṇī.*

[18] The relevant sections are assembled and evaluated in O. Stein, *Arthaśāstra*

the Arthaśāstra can hardly be considered to be the direct source of the medieval architectural handbooks, even if the terminology frequently finds correspondences. Both teaching systems seem to have derived their information independently from each other from the same sources, and fashioned it for their own purposes. Medieval manuals on architecture contain a great deal of information from their own time that is woven with what has been handed down. There are several descriptions of their sections on urban building[19]. These are, however, of little use for a real understanding of the situation one or two thousand years earlier.

For this reason the information from the Arthaśāstra is even more important. The traditional attribution of the authorship to the minister Kauṭilya is hardly historical, and the compendium probably arose in the first half of the first millennium AD. Most of its substantial accounts, however, derive from older handbooks. Clearly, the intention of a compendium on statecraft is to present passages from the older handbooks that are tailored to the needs of the state government: only such facts are dealt with that are relevant for the building authority of the state, while individual questions regarding the construction that are important only to architects are omitted. The 4th chapter of the 2nd book, which is devoted to the planning of a city, thus deals with the number of gates, as well as the number and size of the streets, in summary fashion, before moving on to a detailed account on the planning of the royal residence. With regard to the planning and construction of dwellings we learn nothing. Their construction was not regulated by the state, but was rather a private affair. When in the 3rd book (Ch. 8) private buildings enter into the discussion, however, this is cast exclusively in the context of neighborhood law, with proper regard to public safety and hygiene while determining property borders, fireplaces, and drainage pits.

Even with regard to public edifices such as treasuries, storehouses for material and food, arsenals, and prisons, what is discussed is not the construction in general but rather the planning of the necessary security preparations.[20] The limit placed on description within the scope of a handbook on statecraft is

and Śilpaśāstra, Arch. Or. 7, Prague 1935, p. 473-78; 1936, p. 69-90, p. 334-56; 10, 1938, p. 163-209.

[19] Cf. D.N. Shukla, *Vāstu-Śāstra, Vol. I, Hindu Science of Architecture*, Chandigarh 1960, Part II: *Canons of Town Planning in India and Origins and Growth of Indian Towns*, p. 229-300; B.B. Dutt, *Town Planning in Ancient India*, Calcutta 1925; K. Krishna Murthy, *Town Planning in Ancient India*, JAHRS XXVII, 1961/62, p. 164-70.

[20] Cf. D. Schlingloff, "*Bhūmigṛha*", *JOIB* XVII, 1968, p. 345-52.

the reason why it is difficult to understand many a detail because we do not know their context. This goes especially for the most important contribution to city planning, the chapter regarding the defenses. In our purposes we need not delve into the detailed instructions on the building of towers and gates as they are discussed in Ch. 2.[21] Most important for the overall picture of the city presented in the Arthaśāstra are the specifications regarding moats, ramparts, and walls (see Ch. 2, Figs. 1-9). The earth excavated from three parallel moats[22] close to each other is used for a rampart behind them rising to a height of 10 m.[23] Atop the compressed earth rampart, on which is planted thorn bushes and poisonous plants, stands a wall 5 to 10 m high and half as wide. It is built of brick or stone,[24] interrupted at regular intervals of 54 m by towers quadratic in section, as well as by city gates. The number of city gates is cited in the following chapter in connection with the laying out of the main streets: three main streets are to run from east to west, and three from south to north. Thus, the city had twelve gates.[25] This information regarding the 12 gates is repeated in medieval architectural manuals,[26] which, however, also describe cities with eight and four gate. In a stereotypical way, the narrative literature characterizes a city as having four gates, one at each cardinal direction. [27]

Were we now to attempt to verify the literary picture of the old Indian city by means of actual excavated remains, we must be aware of the preliminary nature of the results. The archaeology of India is still at an early stage. Even if, fortunately, in recent years numerous stratigraphic investigations have contributed substantially to the dating and periodization of urban cultures, large-scale horizontal excavations that might shed light on city planning and the manner of house building are almost completely lacking. Nonetheless, conclusions regarding the layout can be drawn by means of many old cities that have not yet been excavated. As early as the 19th century, Alexander Cunningham made precise outline drawings of numerous cities.[28] Such topographic images

[21] Below, Ch. 2, p. 69f.

[22] See Ch. 2, p. 59f.

[23] Ch. 2, p. 63f.

[24] Ch. 2, p. 65f.

[25] KA. 2,4,1-2: *trayaḥ prācinā rāja-mārgās traya udīcīnā iti vāstu-vibhāgaḥ sa dvādaśa-dvāraḥ*, "...three royal streets oriented to the east, three oriented north: This is the division of the building site. It has twelve gates."

[26] Cf. Stein, loc. cit. Vol. VIII, p. 70, 339.

[27] Even the 64-gate Pāṭaliputra is referred to in Divy. p. 373 and Samantapāsādikā I, p. 52 as a city with four gates.

[28] Reproduced in the *Reports of the Archaeological Survey of India*, Vols. 1-23, 1871-1887 (ASIR).

were only possible because the ruin fields of cities even today are marked by the remains of old city ramparts. From deep breaks in the ramparts one can surmise the position of city gates — not always with complete certainty for streams and artificial landscaping can cause such gaps. Certainly ground-plans allow the calculation of circumference and area of the different cities.

With ingenious perspicacity Cunningham identified in the ruins of cities that he investigated most of the sites mentioned in reports by Chinese pilgrims to India. Inscriptions that came to light in later excavations showed that fewer of his identifications had been erroneous than scholars, from time to time, had previously estimated. Today, few large city ruins exist for which the ancient names remain unknown. An overview of the hitherto topographically recorded cities in order of their size reveals the following picture.[29]

The largest of the ruins visible on the surface lies on the left bank of the Yamunā (Jumna) between the two villages Kosam Inam and Kosam Khiraj, 50 km southwest of Allahabad. As early as 1892 Cunningham identified this site as the well-known capital of the Vatsa land, Kauśāmbī,[30] known from literature as the seat of government of the legendary ruler Udayana,[31] a contem-

[29] The following footnotes contain the archaeological publications to the respective cites; one can omit a documentation of the literary citations of the different city names since these can readily be looked up in dictionaries on ancient Indian Geography. See, among others, N. Dey, *Geographical Dictionary of Ancient and Mediaeval India,* Calcutta 1899 (= Suppl. Ind. Ant. 52, 53, 54, 1923-25); K.D. Bajpai, *The Geographical Encyclopaedia of Ancient and Medieval India,* Varanasi 1967ff.; B.C. Law, *Historical Geography of Ancient and Mediaeval India,* Paris 1954. B.C. Law also has written monographs on nearly all known cities that discuss the literary sources. The city names in Buddhist Pāli texts are collected in G.P. Malalasekara, *Dictionary of Pāli Proper Names,* 2 Vols., London 1937/38; in the Mahābhāṣya, by P.V. Kane, *Ancient Cities and Towns mentioned in the Mahābhāṣya,* JBBRAS, NS 27, 1951/52, p. 38-42. The books by B.N. Puri, *Cities of Ancient India,* Meerut 1966; A. Ray, *Villages, Towns and Secular Buildings in Ancient India,* Calcutta 1964; R.S. Sharma, *Urban Decay in India,* Delhi 1987; and A. Ghosh, *The City in Early Historic India,* Simla 1973, present collections of literary and archaeological notices. For more recent literature, see K.T.S. Sarao, *Urban Centres and Urbanisation as Reflected in the Pāli Vinaya and Sutta Piṭakas,* Ph.D. diss., Cambridge 1989, Bibliography, p. 187-206.

[30] ASIR 1, 1871, p. 301-12; 10, 1880, p. 1-5; 21, 1885, p. 1-3; ARASI 1913/14, p. 261ff.; 1921/22, p. 45-46; Ind. Arch. 1953/54, p. 9; 1954/55, p. 16-17; 1955/56, p. 20-22; 1956/57, p. 28-29; 1957/58, p. 47-49; 1958/59, p. 46-47; 1959/60, p. 46; 1960/61, p. 33-35; 1961/62, p. 50-52; 1962/63, p. 32-33; 1963/64, p. 40; ABIA XVI, 1958, p. xxxvi-xlv; G.R. Sharma, *The Excavations at Kausambi* (1957-59), Allahabad University Publication No 1, Allahabad 1960; Id., *Kausambi,* MASI 74 (1969).

[31] Regarding the Udayana legend, see S. Vrat, *The Story of Udayana and Vāsavadattā through the Ages,* BV 16, 1956, p. 37-45; E. Waldschmidt, *Ein Textbeitrag zur Udayana-Legende,* NAWG, Phil. Hist. Kl. 1968, p. 101-25.

porary of the Buddha. Because this identification conflicts with the distance given by the Chinese pilgrim to India, Hiuen-Tsang, this identification has been subsequently contested. Inscriptions found more recently, however, lend strong confirmation to Cunningham's identification. In 1951 behind the southwestern city gate a monastery was cleared. A seal inscription demonstrated that it was the Ghoṣitārāma cloister,[32] one of the best known monasteries in the Buddhist literature.

Ghoṣaka, the banker of king Udayana, is believed to have founded it. Hiuen-Tsiang described the monastery as lying in the southeastern part of the city,[33] which accords with the archaeological findings. Since 1949, under the aegis of Allahabad University, Kauśāmbī has being excavated systematically. The most important results of these excavations were the layout of the ramparts and the defenses of the southeastern city gate, and the clearing of a *śyenaciti* in front of this gate.[34] The ground plan (Fig. 1) shows a nearly square cityscape bordered by an earthen rampart. Excavations have shown that this rampart was nearly 13 m in height and was encased with 154 layers of brick. Although a wall atop the rampart is yet to be proven, at the foot a moat exists with an enormous width of 145 m that directed the river around the city. The rampart encloses a city area of 2.29 km². Gaps in the rampart point to the existence of six city gates, two on either side on the landside, of which the southeastern one has been excavated. The building of the complex falls in the first half of the 1st century BCE. For a more exact dating one must be a bit patient. It is, however, clear that Kauśāmbī is one of the oldest Indo-Aryan cities. Its size is a sign of the city's importance as a key center of traffic on the trade route between Panjab, through Pāṭaliputra, to the harbor Tāmralipti on the Gulf of Bengal.

On the western bank of an old riverbed of the Yamunā lie the ruins of Sugh (Fig. 2) that Cunningham identified with the royal city Śrughna[35] mentioned in the Mahābhārata and in the report of the pilgrim Hiuen-Tsiang. Its area comprises 1.97 km². On the northern and western sides, which are not bordered by a river bank, Cunningham found depressions in the earth resulting from the city moat. In 1962 excavations took place here. From the fact

[32] ABIA XVI 1958, xliv: *Kauśambyāṃ Ghoṣitārāma-mahā-vihāre bhikṣu-saṅghasya*, "(Seal) of the monks' congregation in the great monastery Ghoṣitārāma in Kauśāmbī."

[33] Transl. Beal, Vol. I, p. 236.

[34] Cf., however, D. Schlingloff, *Menschenopfer in Kauśāmbī?*, IIJ XI, 1969, p. 175-89; B.B. Lal, *The so-called Śyenaciti at Kausambi: A fallen brick-mass*, Purātattva 15, 1986, p. 94ff.

[35] ASIR 2, 1872, p. 226-31; Ind. Arch. 1963/64, p. 27f.

that the city is not mentioned in the old Buddhist texts one may conclude that it does not belong to the group of the oldest Indo-Aryan cities.

Rājagṛha[36] (present-day Rajgir), the old capital of Magadha, has become famous as the site for endless Buddhist and Jaina tales. Different from the other ancient Indian capitals, Rājagṛha was not located in the plane on a riverbank, but rather in a valley surrounded by mountains (Fig. 3). On these mountain crests large sections of a wall of unworked stone is still preserved. At strategically important points, watch towers complement it. The city itself was fortified by means of a rampart of earth strengthened by a core of quarried stone. This rampart encloses an irregularly formed city area of 1.87 km^2. The remains of the northern city gate is preserved; through it the road led to the (New) Rājagṛha at a distance of 1.2 km. New Rājagṛha lies outside of the valley and comprises less than $\frac{1}{7}$ of the surface of the old city (0.25 km^2). A trench or moat and a rampart over 7 m high, upon which a 3.35 m wide brick wall was built, enclose the city in the form of an irregular square. Tradition has it that the new city was founded as early as the time of the Buddha. In reality, however, its origin may be from a much later period,[37] while more recent research in (old) Rājagṛha confirms that this city belonged to the oldest period of Indo Aryan settlements.

Vidiśā,[38] the capital of the Daśārṇa people, became famous as the residence of Agnimitra in one of Kālidāsa's dramas. This city is first mentioned in an inscription of Aśoka in the 3rd century BCE. It lies along an important traffic artery, the rout from the Panjab, through Ujjayinī, to the harbor Bhārukaccha (Broach). With regard to the area, the ruins of this city are only a little smaller than those of Kauśāmbī. They lie at the confluence of the present-day river Bes with the Vetravatī (today: Betva), not far from famous

[36] ASIR 1, 1871, p. 20-27; 3, p. 140-44; 8, p. 85-101; ARASI 1905/06, p. 86-106; 1913/14, p. 265-71; 1925/26, p. 121-27; 1930/34, p. 30-31; 1935/36, p. 52-54; AI 7, 1951, p. 66-78; Ind. Arch. 1953/54, p. 9; 1954/55, p. 16; 1957/58, p. 11; 1958/59, p. 13; 1961/62, p. 6-8; 1962/63, p. 5f.; ARASI Eastern Circle 1905/06, p. 13-15; IA 30, 1901, p. 54-63, 81-97; JBORS 4, 1918, p. 113-35; 5, 1919, p. 331-43; JASB, NS 15, 1949, p. 65-80; Patil, p. 432-72.

[37] See Ind. Arch. 1962/63, p. 5: "The occurrence of the Northern Black Polished Ware in the earliest (pre-rampart) levels was duly confirmed. It is interesting to n. that Carbon 14 determination of the charcoal samples from the pre-rampart layers indicates a date of 245 $\pm$ 105 B.C." [There are two 14C determinations from here with the same published values: TF-45 & TF-46=2150$\pm$100 BP (5568 BP) calibrates to 365 BCE.]

[38] ASIR 10, 1880, p. 36-46; ARASI 1908/09, p. 126 -29; 1913/14, p. 186-226; 1914/15 p. 66-88; Ind. Arch. 1963/64, p. 16f. 1964/65, p. 19f.; 1975/76, p. 30f.; 1976/77, p. 33f.

Buddhist site of Sanci. In 1874 Cunningham recorded the remains of a city rampart preserved to a height of 10 m and a moat that connected the two rivers along the western city border. By means of this moat "the capital city named Vidiśā was surrounded by the Vetravatī" as we learn from a later text.[39] According to Cunningham's drawing the city had a circumference of 5.4 km and a surface area of 1.72 km^2. Roughly rectangular in plan, no one can be certain to what extent the river erosion obscured the old city borders (Fig. 4).

Ahicchatra[40] (in inscriptions Adhicchatra), the capital of the northern Pañcāla famous in the Mahābhārata epic, lies in the Bareli district, U.P., ½ km northeast of the village of Ramnagar. The rampart encloses a city area of 1.52 km^2, in the form of a rather irregular triangle (Fig. 5). During the Islamic period the defensive complex was rebuilt, and thus we cannot tell much about the size and position of the old city gates. Excavations have shown that the city was founded in a time prior to 300 BCE.

Aside from Rājagṛha, the most important site of the Buddha's activities was Śrāvastī,[41] the capital of the kingdom of Kosala, located on the bank of the Aciravatī. Right in front of the city gates, the Jetavana monastery is the scene of events in innumerable Buddhist texts. In 1862 Cunningham identified the ruins of Maheth, which were located along an old course of the Rapti, with Śrāvastī and the neighboring Saheth with the Jetavana monastery. These identifications, which were partially subject to doubt, were confirmed a few years ago by newly found inscriptions. While excavation at Saheth brought to light an extensive monastery, that of a ruin in Maheth illustrated a typical fortified city (Fig. 6). An earthen rampart, preserved to a height of 19 m, bears a 2.75 m wall at its crest and encloses a city area of 1.45 km^2. In all, the rampart evidences 28 depressions, which the locals designate as "gates". But only some of the breaks are really gates. One, the Nausahra gate, was cleared in 1907. Recent archaeological investigations revealed a settlement site that predated the erection of the rampart.

[39] Kād. p. 11: *Vetravatyā parigatā Vidiśābhidhāna-nagarī rājadhāny āsīt.*

[40] ASIR 1, 1871, p. 255-65; Progress Report of the Epigraphical and Architectural Branches of the N.-W. Provinces and Oudh, 1891/92, p. 1ff.; A. Ghosh and K.C. Panigrahi, *Pottery of Ahichchhatra*, AI 1, 1946, p. 37-59 (introduction by A. Ghosh regarding excavations in *A.*); Ind. Arch. 1963/64, p. 43f.

[41] ASIR 1, 1871, p. 330-48; 11, 1880, p. 78-100; JASB 61, 1892, pt. 1, extra number, pl. I-XXX; ARASI 1907/08, p. 81-131; 1908/09, p. 133-38; 1910/11, p. 1-24; Ind. Arch. 1958/59, p. 47; K.K. Sinha, *Excavations at Sravasti*, 1959, Varanasi 1967.

Puṇḍravardhana,[42] capital of the Puṇḍras, a tribe known even from Vedic times, appears in inscriptions and in later texts. In accordance with Cunningham's identification, confirmed by inscriptions, this site is represented by Mahasthangarh in the Bogra district of northern Bengal (in present-day Bangladesh). Couched on the right bank of the Karatoya river (Fig. 7), the site encompasses an area of 1.37 km^2 and is somewhat rectangular in shape. According to Cunningham's investigations, the site was enclosed by a moat and may have had two city gates on each site. Later excavations yielded two temple complexes of early medieval date, which probably hearken back to earlier structures.

On the right bank of the Bhargaui river in Orissa, 2 km southeast of Bhubaneshwar, lies a large ruined area of a city, 1.36 km^2 in extent, which is named after the village of Sisupalgarh located in the interior. A stately clay rampart around 8 m in height encloses the square complex (Fig. 8). Bastions on the four corners and eight gates opening toward the outside, two on each flank, strengthen the impression that we are dealing with a meticulously planned fortress. Excavations in 1946[43] cleared one of these gates and brought to light on the rampart a 3 m wide wall. The earliest settlement of this place begins around 300 BCE. The rampart may have been built a century later, and the wall that is preserved comes from a still later period. In the Hathigumpha cave, 8 km northwest of Sisupalgarh, an inscription of king Khāravela mentions the repair of a gate and rampart of the fort Kaliṅganagara, and one can assume that this was the old name of the city. Excavation began again in 2003 in the center and northern gate.

Periplus Maris Erythraei of the 1st century CE mentions that on the way to the harbor city Barygaza (=Bhārukaccha) on the Gulf of Cambay there was the old royal city Ozene.[44] This Ozene, which Ptolemy names Ozoamis, is identical with the famous Ujjayinī, the capital of Avanti. The city was said to be the residence of the king Pradyota at the time of the Buddha. In the 3rd century BCE, Aśoka resided there as the crown prince, and in the 5th century CE the poet Kālidāsa praised the city in his "Cloud Messenger". The ruins of old Ujjayinī are represented by the

[42] ASIR 15, p. 104-17; ARASI 1928/29, p. 88-97; 1930/34, p. 128f.; 1934/35, p. 40-41; A. Banerji, *Mahasthangarh,* MR 61, 1938, p. 198-201.

[43] B.B. Lal, *Śiśupālgarh 1948: An Early Historical Fort in Eastern India,* AI 5, 1949, 62-105; T.N. Ramachandran, *Śiśupālgarh,* JAHRS 19, 1948, p. 140-53, 1 plate; P. Yule and W. Böhler, *Śiśupalgarh: An Early Historic Fortress in Coastal Orissa and its Cousins,* Beiträge zur allgemeinen und vergleichenden Archäologie 24, 2004, p. 15-29 + CD ROM.

[44] §47; cf. P.H.L. Eggermont, *The Murundas and the Ancient Trade-Route from Taxila to Ujjain,* JESHO 9, 1966, p. 257ff.

Garh Kalika hill on the bank of the Śiprā, north of the modern city of Ujjain. A rampart over 12 m high encompasses the city area of 0.875 km,[45] irregularly pentagonal in shape (Fig. 9). The city defenses predate the first period of settlement in 600 BCE. Eight breaks at irregular intervals probably represent the city gates. A wall on top of the ramparts has not yet been identified. On the other hand, archaeological investigations determined a river-fed moat around the city, 45 m wide and 6.6 m deep. Excavation at Ujjayinī yielded a spectrum of crafted objects, which confirm the reputation of the city as a craft and trade center.

Kānyakubja,[46] today's Kanauj, lies on the west bank of Kālīnādi in Uttar Pradesh. It was the seat of government of Harṣa, the famous 7th-century CE king. The name of the city is recorded in documents as early as the old Buddhist texts. However, excavations have not been conducted that would confirm the age of the site. To judge from Cunningham's drawing, the city was triangular in shape and encompassed a surface of 0.69 km^2 (Fig. 10).

In the early 1960s archaeologists investigated the ruins of a small fortified city, Balirajgarh,[47] whose ancient name is unknown, 80 km northeast of Darbhanga in northern Bihar. The city wall, which dates approximately to the 2nd century CE, encloses a quadrangular city area of 0.45 km^2 and seems to have had four gates (Fig. 11).

The famous Buddhist site of Nagarjunakonda[48] lies on the east bank of the Kṛṣṇā (today: Kistna) in Andhra Pradesh. A small fortified city forms its center, the name of which, Vijayapurī, has come down in inscriptions. Its western border runs at a distance of approximately 100 m from the riverbank and to the south encloses a mountain of 0.12 km^2 in the city area. Atop the city defenses is located a 3-5 m thick wall. In the parts that lay in the valley, a 20-24 m wide moat encircles the fortification. The rampart encloses a city of 0.42 km^2 and has two recognizable main gates, one each on the east and west sides, as well as a small secondary gate on the north side (Fig. 12). The excavations brought to light not only the Buddhist monuments, but also Brahmanic

[45] Ind. Arch. 1955/56, 19f.; 1956/57, 20-28; 1957/58, 32-36; N.R. Banerjee, *The Excavations at Ujjain*, Indologen-Tagung, Göttingen 1960, p. 74-86.

[46] ASIR 1, 1871, p. 279-93.

[47] Ind. Arch. 1962/63, p. 4-5.

[48] ARASI 1926/27, p. 156-61; 1927/28, p. 118-21; 1928/29, p. 100-04; 1929/30, p. 144-51; 1930/34, p. 107-11; T.N. Ramachandran, *Excavations at Nāgārjunakoṇḍa*, IHQ 28, 1952, p. 107-22; Ind. Arch. 1954/55, p. 22f.; 1955/56, p. 23-26; 1956/57, p. 35-38; 1957/58, p. 5-9; 1958/59, p. 5-10; 1959/60, p. 5-10; A. H. Longhurst, *The Buddhist Antiquities of Nāgārjunakoṇḍā, Madras Presidency*, MASI 54, 1938; T.N. Ramachandran, *Nāgārjunakoṇḍā 1938*, MASI 71, 1953.

and secular antiquities: on the river bank column halls[49] and stair structures, in the city remains of wall and streets, a gold smithery, and two ponds for cultic baths. From as early as prehistoric times, the area of Nagarjunakonda was inhabited. The city Vijayapurī itself seems to have flourished in the 2nd-3rd century CE under the Ikṣvāku rulers.

South of the Yamunā (Jumna), about 16 km south-southwest of Allahabad, lie the ruins of Bhita,[50] a small fortified city with a surface area of 0.26 km² (Fig. 13). The excavations of J. Marshall in 1909-12 brought approximately 1.5% of the city surface to light. Thus Bhita is one of the best-known old Indian cities. Aside from the excavation of some houses, important seals and seal inscriptions came to light. Since one of the seals bore the place-name Vichī and a seal impression the name Vichīgrāma, one can assume that this was the name of the place. The rampart, about 12 m high, bore a 3.4 m-thick wall. The number of gates cannot be determined with certainty. The excavations revealed the southeastern city gate and a square defensive tower 55 m away from it. According to Marshall's results, none of the excavated buildings can predate the 4th century BCE. The founding of the city, therefore, does not appear to belong to the oldest period.

In the Champaran district of Bihar, about 2 km southwest of the Aśoka column and the burial mounds of Lauriya, a small fortified city settlement is located, today called Nandangarh.[51] The square-shaped city is 0.2 km² in area (Fig. 14). A stūpa-hill rises in the northeast corner in which were uncovered artifacts of the 1st century BCE, as well as a copper vessel together with a Buddhist birch bark manuscript of the 4th century CE. The name and date of the city remain unknown.

The old name of Eran,[52] located on the southern bank of the Veṇā (today Bina) in Madhya Pradesh, is identified in inscriptions as Airikina, Erakaina, and Erakanya. Excavation in the early 1960s brought to light city defenses with a moat 36 m wide and 8 m deep. Cunningham's old ground plan shows the city to lie in a river meander with an area frequently of 0.18 km² (Fig. 15).

[49] Cf. p. 47, note 165.

[50] ASIR 8, 1873, p. 46-62; 10, 1880, p. 5-6; ARASI 1909/10, p. 40-42; 1911/12, p. 29-94; J. Marshall, *Archaeological Explorations in India 1909-10*, JRAS 1911, p. 127-41.

[51] ASIR 1, 1871, p. 68-74; 16, p. 104-09; 22, p. 36-50; ARASI 1904/05, p. 38-40; 1906/07, p. 119 -26; 1935/36, p. 55 -66; 1936/37, p. 47-50; Patil p. 234-44; J.E. van Lohuizen-de-Leeuw, *South-East Asian Architecture and the Stūpa of Nandangaṛh*, Art. As. XIX, 1956, p. 279-90.

[52] ASIR 10, 1880, p. 76-90; Ind. Arch. 1960/61, p. 17f.; 1961/62, p. 24f.; 1962/63, p. 11f.; 1963/64, p. 15f.; 1964/65, p. 16-18.

Buddhist and Jaina literature frequently mention Vaiśālī,[53] the residence of the Licchavis and the birthplace of the Jaina saint Mahāvīra. It is located 3 km northwest of Basarh in the Muzaffarpur district. With a surface area of 0.14 km^2, it is the smallest of the cities considered here. Therefore, one assumes that the defensive wall does does enclose the city, but only a citadel. Reportedly, the remains of a second, larger fortification is visible.[54] Whether this assumption really holds must be confirmed archaeologically. The area enclosed by the rampart is not small to the extent that it is not comparable with that of the other small cities, and the form of the fortification corresponds closely to that of the other cities. A moat up to 38 m in width and a rampart, on which late a wall was built, enclose a rectangular city surface (Fig. 16). Numerous sanctuaries in the area, some of which have been excavated, substantiate the reputation that the city had, despite its modest size.

Unfortunately, not all of the cities known from the old Indian literature and from archaeology can be determined in terms of their form and surface area. The old borders of many cities are no longer recognizable. The old settlements either are partly or entirely buried by successor cities, or they may have been destroyed by human activity; floods or other natural catastrophes may also have obscured their borders. The most impressive example of a settlement destroyed by a flood is the royal city of Hastināpura. Following the literary tradition, in the 7th generation after the events represented in the epic Mahābhārata, the Ganges destroyed the city, and the seat of government was moved to Kauśāmbī.[55] The 1951/52 excavations of the ruin mound near the present-day village of Hastināpur[56], on an old arm of the Ganges, proved the destruction caused by a flood that made the place uninhabitable for some time. Led by the seem-

[53] ASIR 1, 1871, p. 55-64; 16, p. 6-12, 89-91; ARASI 1903/04, p. 81-122; 1911/12, p. 18f.; 1913/14, p. 98-155; Ind. Arch. 1957/58, p. 10f.; 1958/59, p. 12; 1959/60, p. 14-16; 1960/61, p. 6; 1961/62, p. 5f.; ASI, Eastern Circle, Rep. 1911/12, 48-52; Krishna Deva and Mishra Vijayakanta, *Vaiśālī Excavations,* Vaiśālī 1961; B.P. Sinha and S.R. Roy, *Vaisāli excavations: 1958-62,* Patna 1969; Patil p. 21-36.

[54] *Vaiśālī Excavations,* p. 1: "Rājā-Viśāla-kā Garh citadel ... The remains of a second and much larger city-wall have been traced extending in a straight line over a length of more than a mile running from the present village of Konsā to Dharārā, situated about half a mile south of Rājā-Viśāla-kā-Garh."

[55] Viṣṇupurāṇa, pt. IV, ch. 21: *nṛpaḥ Gaṅgayāpahṛte tasmin nagare Nāga-sāhvaye tyaktvā Nicakṣur nagaraṃ Kauśāmbyāṃ sa nivatsyati.* "If the Ganges will have washed away this 'elephant' (*nāga* = *hastin*) named city and the king Nicakṣu will have left the city, he will settle in Kauśāmbī."

[56] B.B. Lal, *New Light on the "Dark Age" of Indian History: Recent Excavations at the Hastināpura Site, Near Delhi,* Illustrated London News, Oct. 4, 1962, p. 551-53; B.B. Lal, *Excavations at Hastināpura and other Explorations in the Upper Gangā and Sutlej Basins 1950-52,* AI 10/11, 1954/55, p. 5-151; A. Chand, *Hastināpura, The Glory of Ancient India,* Banares 1952.

ing great age of the events recounted in the epic, archaeologists dated this catastrophe to a very early period. A C14 assay shows, however, that this event cannot have taken place prior to 335±115 BCE (uncalibrated).[57] Following rebuilding, the city was again destroyed, this time as a result of a fiery conflagration. Although again rebuilt, the city was given up soon afterwards and remained unsettled into the medieval period. As in few other excavation sites, the stratigraphic investigations at Hastināpura have revealed a dynamic history. Especially here, it is time for horizontal clearance, which is bound to yield rich results; for it is not times of peaceful settlement that give the best archaeological results, but rather catastrophes that force inhabitants to save their valuables.

From the Mahābhārata, the equally famous royal city Indraprastha preserves its name in Indarpat, a designation of the Islamic "Old Fort" (Purāna Qila) on the western bank of the Yamunā near the center of Delhi. Even if Cunningham was of the opinion that not a single stone of the old city of Yudhiṣṭhira was still to be found,[58] excavations[59] have shown that the site was settled as early as the Indo-Aryan founding of cities. In the later periods the buildings were made of baked brick.

Vārāṇasī (old Benares) is represented by Rajghat, a ruin 18 m high on the left bank of the Ganges, northeast of the present-day city.[60] Excavations have brought to light the remains of a fortification on the riverbank in the form of a rampart that belongs to the earliest period of habitation. Further details with regard to the location and course of this rampart remain unpublished.

Mention is made of mud ramparts around Mathurā, the old city of artists and craftsmen, which lies mostly beneath today's city of the same name on the right bank of the Yamunā. But more detailed information on this is available. Finds excavated[61] from the Katra hill show that Mathurā also belongs to the oldest group of settlement sites.

Stratigraphic investigations, which yield numerous single finds in addition to a valuable periodization, have been carried

[57] Cf. B.B. Lal in AI 18/19, 1962/63, p. 221: "The Hastināpura samples from the upper levels of the Painted Grey Ware Culture, range in date from 505 ±130 B.C. to 335 ±115 B.C. [uncalibrated, our brackets]. This brings down, by about three centuries, the dating suggested by the present writer and upholds the one put forward by Sir Mortimer Wheeler. The Hastināpura samples were reported to be mixed with rootlets. Thus, before adopting the new dates finally, it would perhaps be worth while to await determinations from other Painted Grey Ware sites."

[58] ASIR 1, 1871, p. 135-36.

[59] Ind. Arch. 1954/55, p. 13-14.

[60] ASIR 1, 1871, p. 103ff.; Ind. Arch. 1957/58, p. 50f.; 1960/61, p. 35-39; 1961/62, p. 57-59; 1962/63, p. 41; 1963/64, p. 58f.

[61] Ind. Arch. 1954/55, p. 15f.

out in several other sites. Here I want to mention the excavations carried out in Tāmralipti (Tamluk),[62] Chandraketugarh,[63] Madhyamika (Nagari),[64] Amreli,[65] Kauṇḍinyapura,[66] Māhiṣmatī (Maheshwar),[67] Nasik,[68] Kolhapur,[69] and the like. Till now these excavations have produced no information with regard to the cityscape, size, and fortifications. However, archaeological research in India is advanced to the point that few of the sites mentioned in the old Indian literature are not identified.

Thus, there is good reason to consider the known sites to be representative of the old Indian city *per se*. Indeed, we can point to a series of attributes that these cities hold in common. With the exception of old Rājagṛha, all of the cities lie in the plains near rivers. Water supplied by rivers flows around the cities in a wide moat. The earth dug from the moat provides the material to build the rampart. As well as we can tell, a wall was erected on top of the rampart during a later building period. With regard to the moats, ramparts, and walls, the city defenses correspond to the directives of the Arthaśāstra. In this work the *status quo* is given normative expression.

The Indian method of fortification differs essentially from the Greek one with only a wall. This type of fortification is documented in the region of India in two later city complexes at Taxila: Sirkap and Sirsukh. Taxila[70] (Skt. Takṣaśilā) was a nodal point for communication on the route between West and Central Asia, and

[62] ARASI 1921/22, p. 74f.; Ind. Arch. 1954/55, p. 19f.; T.N. Ramachandran, *'Tāmraliptī (Tamluk)'*, Art. As. 14, 1951, p. 226-239.

[63] Ind. Arch. 1956/57, p. 29f.; 1957/58, p. 51-53; 1958/59, p. 55f.; 1959/60, p. 50-52; 1960/61, 39; 1961/62, p. 62f.; 1962/63, p. 46f.; 1963/64, p. 63ff.

[64] ASIR 6, 1878, p. 197-226; D.R. Bhandarkar, *Archaeological Remains and Excavations at Nagari*, MASI 4, 1920; Ind. Arch. 1962/63, p. 19f.; U. P. Shah and R. N. Mehta, *Nagara (An early Historic site)*, JOIB 12, 1963, p. 403-06.

[65] S.R. Rao, *Excavations at Amreli, A Kshatrapa-Gupta Town*, Museum and Picture Gallery, Bulletin Vol. XVIII, 1966.

[66] Ind. Arch. 1961/62, 29f.; M.G. Dikshit, *Excavations at Kaundinyapura*, Bombay 1968.

[67] H.D. Sankalia, B. Subbarao, S.B. Deo, *The Excavations at Maheshwar and Navdatoli 1952-53*, Deccan College Research and M. S. University Publication No. 1, Poona 1958.

[68] H.D. Sankalia and S.B. Deo, *Report on the Excavations at Nasik and Jorwe 1950-51*, Deccan College Monograph Series No. 13, Poona 1955.

[69] H.D. Sankalia and M.G. Dikshit, *Excavations at Brahmapuri (Kolhapur) 1945-46*, Deccan College Monograph Series 5, Poona 1952.

[70] Cf. J. Marshall, *Taxila, An illustrated account of archaeological excavations carried out at Taxila under the orders of the Government of India between the years 1918 and 1934*, 3 volumes, Cambridge 1951. The earlier excavation reports in ASIR, ARASI and MASI are worked into this study. For more recent excavations see: A. Ghosh, *Taxila (Sirkap) 1944-45*, AI 4, 1947/48, p. 41-48; G. M. Young, *A New Hoard from Taxila (Bhir Mound)*, AI 1, 1946, p. 27-36.

from the Indian ports of Bhārukaccha on the Gulf of Cambay and Tāmralipti on the Gulf of Bengal. Lying in the extreme northwest, it was always strongly influenced by cultural elements from outside of India. The non-Indian cityscape makes it clear how problematic it is to interpret the results of the excavation within an Indian context, as in fact happened some time ago.[71] The question to what extent the complex Bhir Mound, the oldest of the three city structures in Taxila (6th century BCE or older), can be understood as a genuine Indian city must remain open for the time being. The city defenses, which are missing in places, according to Marshall, consisted of mud brick and clay together with wood.[72] The houses excavated, as we shall see below, deviate considerably from the developed Indian type of house.

Turning now to the laying out of houses and streets in old Indian cities, again we must turn to the Arthaśāstra, which prescribes a system of three east-west and three north-south streets. This "parceling out the construction ground" (*vāstu-vibhāga* KA. 2,4,1) into a rectangular grid of streets creates uniform living quarters (*bhāga*), which are also characteristic of the Greek "hippodamian" urban constructions. If poetic texts praise the streets as "well-planned" (*su-vibhakta*),[73] they consider as normal a planned city as the Arthaśāstra does. To delve further into this question, unfortunately, few excavated sources are available.

In the Bhir Mound, the oldest settlement in Taxila, approximately 12000 m^2 was cleared (Fig. 17) revealing the opposite of a well-planned settlement. The city plan (Fig. 18) shows twisting streets and alleys that frequently end at small places or as cul de sacs in front of houses. The layout of the streets is just as unplanned as that of the houses, and often it is impossible to determine where one house stops and the next one begins.[74]

[71] H. Scharfe, *Investigations on Kauṭalya's Manual of Political Science*, Wiesbaden 1993, p. 148ff., who builds on O. Stein, Arch Or. 10, 1938, p. 191ff.

[72] Vol. I, p. 3: "in some of these bays, where the soil has been much eroded, it is no longer possible to trace the original position of the city's defences. The walls themselves were built of unbaked brick or mud, supplemented by timber, which has now perished"; 39: "the older mound of beaten earth or unbaked brick which surrounded the Bhiṛ Mound city".

[73] Cf. e.g. Rām. 1,5,8: *rājamārgena ... suvibhaktena*, "with a well laid out royal street"; Rām. 1,5,10 = Ap. 6,87: *suvibhaktāntarāpaṇāṃ*, "(the city) with well-laid out interior shops"; Rām. 5,58,20: *suvibhaktāṃś ca catvarān*, "well laid out cross roads"; Rām. 1,6,8 = 2,45,19 = 3,52,12 = 5,2,47: *suvibhakta-mahāpathāṃ*, "(the city) with well-laid out main paths"; Mbh. 1,199,34: *suvibhakta-mahārathyaṃ*, "(the city) with well-laid out main streets".

[74] Vol. I, p. 92: "The principle underlying their design is the common oriental one of the open court with rooms on one or more sides, but there is so much diversity in the application of this principle and the plans are so chaotic, that it is often impossible to determine where one house ends and another begins."

Excavations of Indian cities yield an entirely different picture. Unfortunately, the report of the excavation from Kauśāmbī is not very precise regarding how the houses are positioned on the street.[75] In Sisupalgarh (above p. 21) the square city plan suggests a parallel layout of the main streets from gate to gate,[76] but hitherto this has not been archaeologically verified.

For this question, the excavations in Bhita are most promising. Here J. Marshall cleared two streets and a few adjacent houses on the southeastern edge of the city (Fig. 19). Apart from certain additions, they date to the first centuries BCE. One of the two streets, which Marshall named "High Street", begins at the city gate and leads straight on to a sanctuary in the center of the city. The second, somewhat smaller, street named "Bastion Street" begins at a defensive tower and continues exactly parallel to the High Street (Fig. 20). The High Street is about 9 m wide, and the Bastion Street is 4 m wide. The houses on Bastion Street are also smaller than those on High Street, but they show the same floor plan. This plan shows a freestanding building with three or more rooms facing the street. At the back lies a court vestibule of about the same width, and further back one finds a square structure that consists of a number of rooms clustered around a courtyard (Figs. 21, 22). This same arrangement of rooms around a courtyard is apparent in some of the houses excavated in (new) Rājagṛha (Fig. 23). It is also observable in *The Excavations at Kauśāmbī.*[77]

Contemporary representations reveal an exact picture of the manner in which such houses were built. The layout of the rooms around an interior courtyard certainly originates in the house-type consisting of four long houses arranged around a farmyard[78] that is represented in reliefs at Bharhut (Fig. 24). With the adoption of this rural house as a city dwelling, the four long houses were set off

[75] ABIA XVI, 1958, p. xxxix: "The houses in this area seem to have been planned along a road."

[76] AI 5, p. 64: "Such a disposition clearly suggests a regular planning not only of the fortifications but presumably also of the streets inside, which are likely to have run east-west and north-south, connecting the opposite gateways in a grid-pattern. "

[77] ABIA XVI, 1958, p. xl: "The plan of the houses is fairly simple. The rooms were built on the four sides of a courtyard, the rooms usually being provided with verandahs around the courtyard. Some of the houses had two sections, the one on the main road or lane possibly meant for the use of males, and the internal one for the use of the women folk. The ceilings of the rooms of the apartments of men folk in certain cases were supported by wooden posts. Unfortunately, our source, G.R. Sharma, reproduces no plan of such house, which is designated as a, "house with two living areas" (*dvivāsagṛha* Kāmas. IV).

[78] Referred to in the literature as *catuḥśāla*; cf. Mbh. 1,132,8: *catuḥśālaṃ gṛhaṃ*; Mbh. 3,204,5: *saudhāṃ... catuḥśālam*; Rām. 2,85,29: *catuḥśālāni śubhrāṇi*; Mṛcch., 1st act: *abbhantaracadussālādo.*

from the street and supplemented on the frontage by a fifth structure. This structure, which in literature is referred to as a reception hall,[79] may have been served as a foyer, or, in commercial streets, it may have served as a shop. Shop fronts facing main streets do not only find mention in the literature,[80] but they are depicted in the wall paintings at Ajanta.[81] In addition, at Ajanta a house is depicted that shows a fifth freestanding building behind four houses that surround an interior court (Fig. 25). This corresponds exactly to the house plan at Bhita. A tree drawn in the space between the foyer and yard suggests that this forecourt was a grove; it is called 'tree garden' in the literature.[82] Visitors must first cross this grove before reaching the yard containing the four long houses.[83] As opposed to the simple rural house, this atrium house was subject to elaboration in different ways. Thus, houses excavated in Bhita and Rājagṛha always have an interior court with a terrace.[84]

[79] *dvāra-koṣṭhaka, dvāra-prakoṣṭha-śālā*; P *dvāra-koṭṭhaka*. Visitors are received in this entrance hall, JM p. 19: *pratyekabuddhas tad-gṛham abhijagāma bhikṣārthī samupetya ca dvāra-koṣṭhake vyatiṣṭhata*; "the Pratyekabuddha went to this house in order to take nourishment; coming closer, he placed himself in the entry hall". Mendicants to whom the keeper does not permit entrance stand in front of the hall: M. 1, p. 382: *dovāriko... Nigaṇṭhaṃ Nātaputtaṃ etad avoca: Tiṭṭha bhante, mā pāvisi... Nigaṇṭho... Nātaputto... bahi-dvāra-koṭṭhake ṭhito*, "the doorman ... spoke to (name): 'Wait, stop, honourable [sir], do not enter' ..., (name)... is standing outside in front of the entry hall'."

[80] See above, p. 14, note 12.

[81] See Ch. 3.

[82] Cf. Kāmas. IV,3: *bhavanam āsannodakaṃ vṛkṣa-vāṭikāvad vibhakta-karma-kakṣaṃ dvivāsa-gṛhaṃ* "a building (*i.e.*) a house with two living areas, near drinking water with a grove of trees and with a yard for work". The next sentence explains that the working yard is used for carving and lathe work, as well as for other playful activities (*takṣatakṣaṇa-sthānam anyāsāṃ ca krīḍānām*), while in the grove a comfortable and well-shaded swing is to be hung (*svāstīrṇā preṅkhā-dolā vṛkṣa-vāṭikāyāṃ sa-pracāyā*).

[83] Also a thief who broke into the house of a merchant takes this way, Mṛcch. 3rd act: *vṛksa-vāṭikāpasare saṃdhiṃ kṛtvā praviṣṭo 'smi madhyamakam, tad yāvad idānīṃ catuḥśālakam api dūṣayāmi*, "after having made a space in the exit of the grove, I crept through the middle. I wanted now to damage the building which consisted of four long houses"; = Cār. 3rd act: *vṛkṣa-vāṭikā-pakṣa-dvāre saṃdhiṃ chitvā praviṣṭo 'smi, tad yāvad idāniṃ catuḥśālam upasarpāmi*, "having beaten a space in the side door of the grove, I crept in. In this way I wanted to sneak into the building, which consisted of four long houses." Also in the first act of Śakuntalā the king entering the hermitage of Kaṇvas first comes in the grove. In Mṛcch. act 6 Maitreya enters the grove in the palace of Vasantasenā after he had passed through eight entry halls *(prakoṣṭha)*. Vasantasenā is imputed fabulous wealth, and her palace instead of having one entry hall has eight. In each of these halls a different group of clients waits.

[84] *vitardi*, Rām. 2,13,25, Pādat. p. 33,12; for further citations, ibid., p. 194. The passage in Harṣac. p. 178,4: *catuḥśāla-vitardikāyāṃ*, "...on the terrace in the building [consisted] of four long houses" proves that *vitardi* designates the terraces that were verified by means of excavations.

The multi-storied building, however, was the most important development of refined urban houses. Marshall showed that the houses in Bhita had at least one upper floor. Finds of numerous seals and impressions show that local business took place in the upper stories.[85] The structure of different stories also can be studied in contemporary depictions. We find in the reliefs from Bharhut and Sanci upper stories and barrel vaulted roofs two to four stories high. Each story is recessed from the one below it. This creates galleries that could be accessed through several large, round arched doors that were framed by arched pediments (Figs. 26, 27).

Despite having many stories, city houses retain the general character of rural houses. Further, the palatial homes of wealthy citizens and even royal residences seem essentially little more than complexes of more than a single rural house. In the epics there is frequent mention of "courts" that a visitor must pass through[86] before he arrives at the private chambers of the royal family within the central court complex.[87] He had to pass three,[88] occasionally seven,[89] courts before entering the royal quarters. In the Arthaśāstra, the king is received in the morning by different persons within the three courts that lie before these quarters.[90]

Because the single rural house conditions the form of the city house, even in the city each house unit retains its character as an individual building. The firewalls of adjacent houses nev-

[85] ARASI 1911/12, p. 31, 36 = JRAS 1911, p. 129.

[86] Rām. 2,15,16: *sa sarvaḥ samatikramya kakṣyā ... śuddhāntaḥpuram abhyagāt*, "after he had crossed all the yards ... he went in the clear interior residence".

[87] Rām. 2,14,321*: *madhyama-kakṣyāyāṃ*; Mbh. 3,71,17: *madhyama-kakṣāyāṃ*. Cf. KA. 1,20,1: *aneka-kakṣyā-parigatam antaḥpuraṃ*, "the royal residence surrounded by several courtyards".

[88] Mbh. 5,89,2-3: *kakṣyā vyatikramya tisro ... prāsādam āruroha*, "after he crossed through three courtyards,... he entered into the palace"; Mbh. 5,87,12: *tisraḥ kakṣyā vyatikramya ... rājānam abhyagacchad*, "after he had crossed through three courtyards,... he went to the king"; Rām. 2,5,4: *sa Rāma-bhavanaṃ prāpya ... tisraḥ kakṣyā rathenaiva viveśa*, "after he reached Rāmas's house,... he passed with his car through three courtyards"; Mbh. 2,19,28: *janākīrṇās tisraḥ kakṣyā*, "three courtyards filled with people".

[89] Rām. 4,82,19: *sa sapta kakṣyā... praviśya... dadarśāntaḥpuram*, "after he seven courtyards... he entered,... he viewed the royal residence" Rām. 2,51,15-20: *kakṣyāḥ saptābhicakrāma ... sa praviśyāṣṭamīṃ kakṣyaṃ*, "he passed through seven courtyards... and entered the eighth courtyard".

[90] KA. 1,21,1: *śayanād utthitaḥ strīgaṇair dhanvibhiḥ parigṛhyeta, dvitīyasyāṃ kakṣyāyāṃ kañcukoṣṇīṣibhir varṣadharābhyāgārikaiḥ, tṛtīyasyāṃ kubja-vāmana-kirātaiḥ, caturthyāṃ mantribhiḥ saṃbandhibhir dauvārikaiś ca prāsa-pāṇibhiḥ*, "Having gotten up from the bed, he should be received by the groups of female archers, in the second courtyard by the chamberlains in gown and turban, in the third by hunchbacks, dwarfs and tribesmen, in the fourth by his advisors and followers, as well as by the lance-bearing gate watchmen."

er jibe together and a narrow alley lies between them. Not only in Bhita but also in other excavations, house remains brought to light such a passage, as at Vaiśālī,[91] Rājagṛha,[92] Kolhapur,[93] Sambhar,[94] Chandravalli,[95] and Sisupalgarh.[96] This practice, therefore, was wide-spread enough that it was also legally regulated: the Vasiṣṭhasmṛti prescribes a three-foot alley between the houses;[97] according to the Arthaśāstra, its width is 24 thumbs or three feet.[98]

This shows that the findings in Bhita may safely be viewed as characteristic of the Indian practice. As opposed to Taxila, in Bhita the clear borderlines between the housing units enable further observations regarding road building. As previously noted, at a distance of 45 m, Bastion Street runs parallel to High Street. Unfortunately, few of the houses between the two streets have been excavated. The houses (including the shops) on the other side of the street are 24 m in length along the High Street and 20 m long along Bastion Street. Assuming the same situation for the other side of the street, then the distance between both streets corresponds to two blocks. Each of these two houses thus had one side facing the street and three sides facing neighboring houses. The arrangement of the houses and streets can only result from exact city planning. Bhita is thus, in fact, a "well laid-out" city as praised in the epic poetry and prescribed as the norm in the Arthaśāstra.

Marshall's excavation in the southeast of Bhita encompasses about 1% of the city. Assuming the same proportion of houses and streets over the entire city, it would have contained about 940 houses. Bearing in mind the living conditions of the age, we can estimate the population density of such a city. As the ancient literature shows, the houses were generally family dwellings. One must estimate that an extended family of the time, with children, grandparents, unmarried uncles and aunts, as well as domestics, comprised around 10-20 persons, who occupied adequately a 2-3-story house with an area of 60 m^2 per floor.

[91] *Vaiśālī Excavations*, Fig. 4: plan of VS II.

[92] ARASI 1905/06, pl. XXXVI, XXXVII.

[93] *Excavations at Brahmapuri (Kolhapur)*, p. 138: "A narrow regular (or irregular) passage of about 2 ft. separated one house from another. They had no common party walls."

[94] *Excavations at Sambhar*, p. 21.

[95] *Excavations at Brahmapuri (Kolhapur)*, p. 138, note 1.

[96] AI 5, 1949, p. 70: "Two adjoining houses, built of laterite blocks and lying north and south, were exposed with a 2-foot wide space between them."

[97] Vas. 16,8: *taruṇa-gṛheṣv arthāntareṣu tripāda-mātram* "Near new-built houses (and) other things (of the same description there shall be) a passage three feet broad" (transl. Bühler, SBE 14, p. 80).

[98] KA. 3,8,18: *sarva-vāstukayoḥ... kiṣkur-antarikā tri-padī vā*, "between all of the properties there should be a space of 24 thumbs or 3 foot".

Under this assumption, ten to twenty thousand people inhabited Bhita. Over three times as large, Ujjayinī had between thirty and sixty thousand inhabitants; and Kauśāmbī, the largest of the cities dealt with here, had a population of ninety to one hundred eigthy thousand. In area the old Indian cities match contemporary cities of Greco-Roman antiquity. Kauśāmbī had about the same surface area as Athens (length of the Themistoclean walls 6.5 km, enclosed area 2.15 km^2), the population of which is estimated to have been 100,000. Śrughna was as large as Roman Augusta Treverorum (Trier), Ujjayinī somewhat smaller than Milet, Jerusalem, or Colonia Agrippinensis (Cologne); Kānyakubja was larger than Pompeii, and Vijayapurī (Nagarjunakonda) as large as Priene or Nida (Heddernheim).

One old Indian city has been excluded from our survey, because, as a result of its size, it is in a class of its own: it is Pāṭaliputra, capital of the Mauryan empire. The Greek Megasthenes, the ambassador of Seleukos Nicator around 300 BCE to the court of Candragupta, the first Maurya ruler in Pāṭaliputra, gave a report of the city in his India Report. Pāṭaliputra lay at the confluence of Ganges and Erannoboas and formed a parallelogram of 80 x 50 Stadia, length to width. It had a defensive palisade with 570 towers, 64 gates, and a city moat six plethra wide and 30 ells deep.[99] According to these data, the city would have had a circumference of 33.8 km and a surface area of about 25.5 km^2. It was over eleven times larger than Kauśāmbī and nearly 100 times larger than Bhita. Pāṭaliputra is by head and shoulders far larger than the largest cities of antiquity. Alexandria comprised only ⅓ the area of Pāṭaliputra, and imperial Rome inside the 18.8 km long Aurelian wall, with an area of 13.72 km^2, was little more than the half its size. Pāṭaliputra was the largest city in antiquity.

Megasthenes's description of the size sounds improbable to the extent that one might question its reliability. One could assume that the diplomat exaggerated in order to place the city where he was posted in as bright a light as possible. One might also assume that Megasthenes could hardly have measured the city wall himself, but rather that he referred to Indian survey data. Now, on the one hand, Indian fantasy in the narrative literature is well known.[100] On the other hand, Megasthenes's reports regard-

[99] Megasthenes' comment occurs in two fragments in Strabo XV,702 and Arrian Ind. X, 2/8), which represent the shorter and longer versions of one and the same account; cf. O. Stein *Megasthenes und Kauṭilya*, p. 80; his text follows the edition of E.A. Schwanbeck, Bonn 1846, p. 307.

[100] Different cities are attributed a length of twelve *yojana* (Rām. 1,5,7; MPS 34,1) and a breadth of seven (MPS 34,1) or three *yojana* (Rām. 1,5,7). If a *yojana* is 7 km in length then the surface of these cities would be 4000 (or 2000) times

ing the road measurements[101] are confirmed by those of Chinese pilgrims.[102] Clearly Indian surveyors were more than storytellers and could measure distances with considerable accuracy. However, the exactness of Megasthenes's measurements is confirmed not by general considerations, but rather by a simple arithmetic operation. According to him 64 gates and 570 towers are distributed over 33,800 m city wall. Accordingly, the tower-to-tower interval measures 53.22 m.[103] This distance corresponds almost exactly to the required 54 m interval between the towers.[104] Ancient poliorketics (sappers) give about the same distance, which represents the optimal distance for the penetration of arrows.[105] The correspondence thus does not depend on the Arthaśāstra regarding the conditions in Pāṭaliputra or on ancient authors, but rather on the general requirements of fortifications. That the relation of the number of towers and wall intervals of Megasthenes corresponds exactly to this law confirms the reliability of his city plan, which we now need only to fix geographically.

Nearly 200 years ago the suspicion first became manifest that Pāṭaliputra was identical with the present-day city of Patna in Bihar on the right bank of the Ganges.[106] Since then, this suspicion has been confirmed by excavations in Patna and the surrounding area. But the exact location of Pāṭaliputra has remained unclear until now. As we shall see, this has led to serious misunderstandings in the interpretation of archaeological contexts. Fixing Pāṭaliputra's location is frought with certain difficulties, but these can be ameliorated. The essential problem is that of the old courses of the river. An old Indian grammatical work mentions that Pāṭaliputra lies along the Śoṇa river,[107] and in a drama

as large on the average as the archaeologically known city areas. Even if the circumference of the wall is given as only twelve *yojana* (Jāt. I, p. 125: *Bārāṇasiyā pākāraparikkhepadvādasayojaniko hoti*), the surface of this city would be 200 times as large as that of Kauśāmbī. That one cannot accept data of this kind for geographic calculations (thus J.F. Fleet, JRAS 1907, p. 641ff.) must be self-evident.

[101] Strabo XV,708: "They [the Agoranoms] produce roads and erect every 10 stadia a column which shows the crossroads and distances" (Stein, p. 18); Strabo XV,707: "Among them [the officials] the [Agoranoms] work on rivers and survey the land as in Egypt" (Stein, p. 22).

[102] Cf. F. Weller, *Yojana und li bei Fa hsien*, ZDMG 74, 1920, p. 225-37.

[103] Stein 36, note 3, in his calculations forgot to include the gates which also count as fortified points as do the towers.

[104] KA. 2,3,10: *triṃśad-daṇḍāntaraṃ*, "with an interval of thiry staff-lengths".

[105] Cf. Vitruvius, *Archit.* I,V,4; ed. C. Festerbusch, p. 56.

[106] James Rennell, *Memoirs of a Map of Hindostan*, London 1783.

[107] Mahābhāṣya, Vol. I, p. 380; *anu Gaṅgaṃ Hāstinapuram anu Gaṅgaṃ Vārāṇasī anu Śoṇaṃ Pāṭaliputram*, "Hāstinapura along the Ganges, Benares along the Ganges, Pāṭaliputra along the Śoṇa."

the war elephants of the besiegers drink from the Śoṇa.[108] But as we noted, Megasthenes gives the position of the city as lying at the confluence of the Ganges and the Erannoboas[109] (=Sanskrit Hiraṇyavāhā). Although Pliny counts the Sonos and Erannoboas as tributaries of the Ganges,[110] there can be little doubt that these are two different names for the same river, because old Indian dictionaries cite the Śoṇa and Hiraṇyavāhā as synonyms.[111] The red shimmering water[112] from which the river derives its name, "the red", in the same way evoked the poetic name "gold stream" for the Hiraṇyavāhā. Nowadays the Son, however, no longer flows into the Ganges near Patna but rather 25 km further west near Dinapur. But geological investigations show that earlier the two rivers joined each other east of present day Patna.[113] Though the position of the old riverbed requires clarification,[114] the information of the Mahābhāṣya that Pāṭaliputra lay "along the Śoṇa river" is just as valid as Megasthenes's mention that the city lay at the confluence of the Erannoboas with the Ganges.

[108] Mudr. 4th act, v. 16, p. 102: *Śoṇaṃ ...mama gaja-patayaḥ pāsyanti śataśaḥ*, "my elephants will drink 100 times from the Śoṇa".

[109] The name Erannoboas only appears in Arrian; Strabo speaks about the confluence of the Ganges and "of the other river".

[110] Pliny, Nat. Hist. VI,22.

[111] Amarakośa I,2,3,33; Śabdaratnākara 691.

[112] Cf. ASIR 8, 1872/73, p. 8: "The Son rises in the highlands of Amarkantak, and flows through a country possessing a reddish gravelly soil. In the floods the river necessarily brings down large volumes of the red dust and sand, which it deposits in the deeper pools."

[113] J.D. Beglar in ASIR 8, 1872/73, p. 7 notes the following regarding the previous course of the Son: "According to my observations then made, and information from competent authority, I consider that at some remote period the Son flowed in a south-east course from the present village of Tarārh near Dāüdnagar, passing close to the village of Rampur-Chai and Kayal, and not far from the great plain (Tanr) of Deokund ... From Kayal I consider it probable that the Son continued in a north-east direction, entering the bed of the present Punpun at the village of Son-Bhadr ... From Son-Bhadr, the Son in olden times appears to have flowed in what is now the bed of the Punpun as far as Sigori, a small village close to the Punpun near Chandos Buzurg ... From here it, or at least a branch, appears to have taken a course due east, crossing over the bed of the present Punpun river to the bed of the present Murhar river ... from here it flowed in the bed of the present Murhar river till it finally joined the Ganges at Fatuha."

[114] If one follows the course of the Son given by Beglar, then the old riverbed would lie 12 km away from Patna. This, however, contradicts the information of the Mahābhāṣya, according to which Pāṭaliputra lies along the Son. In the *Report on Kumrahar Excavations* the appended map, as well as Waddell's map, also designate the land directly south of Patna as the "Old bed of River Sone". It remains, however, unclear whether this information derives from geological investigation. In any case it remains to be investigated whether the artificial groups of mounds 2 km south of Patna (southeast of Kumrahar) lie on the near or far side of the river.

The interpretation of the literary sources sheds further light on the old stream courses. Long ago not only the Son but also the Ganges near Pāṭaliputra must have had different courses. Even Megasthenes's description of the shape of the city makes this clear. The extended, narrow city did not form a rectangle, as one might assume, but rather a parallelogram — a form which would only result from the confluence of two rivers: rivers never meet at a right angle, but rather at an oblique one. Thus, if the Son, which in ancient times ran east-west, bordered the parallelogram Pāṭaliputra on its lower long flank, then the Ganges must have flowed from the northwest toward the southeast. The assumption that the Ganges bordered the city of Pāṭaliputra not only on its eastern narrow flank of the parallelogram, but rather, as in the case of present-day Patna, also on the northern long side, contradicts the information of the Mahābhāṣya. Here Pāṭaliputra is mentioned clearly as lying "along the Śoṇa", while in the case of the cities Hastināpura and Benares, it notes that they lay "along the Ganges". Further evidence against the city being bordered in the north by the Ganges is Megasthenes's mention of the city moat. It would have been senseless to build this mighty moat, 177 m wide, if the Ganges bordered the city on its northern long side and the Śoṇa on its southern side. The moat is readily understandable if only the southern long side and the eastern short side bordered the river. As in the case of other cities, here the river water flowed around the city by means of a moat that surrounded the sides of the city that did not lie on the riverbank. A further reference to the course of the Ganges during that time is to be found in the travelogue of the Chinese pilgrim to India, Fa-hsien. In order to travel from Vaiśālī to Pāṭaliputra, Fa-hsien crossed the Ganges. He reports that he reached a place where five rivers meet. He then crossed a river and arrived at Pāṭaliputra after proceeding a *yojana* (c. 7 km) toward the south.[115] If like present-day Patna, Pāṭaliputra had been situated on the southern bank, the distance of one *yojana* would be incomprehensible. If the river flowed from the northwest to the southeast and touched the city only on its eastern short side, then it seems clear that one crossed the river a few kilometers further north in order to reach the city by the shortest route. As late as the 16th century there is trustworthy documentation that places the city to the west and not south of the Ganges. In 1541, Sher Shah, marching from Bengal, reaches the bank of the Ganges. Seeing the small city Patna, he decides to fit this place with fortifications owing to

[115] *The Travels of Fa-hsien (399-414 A.D.) or Record of the Buddhistic Kingdoms*, retranslated by H.A. Giles, Cambridge 1923, p. 44ff.

its favorable location, "because this place is located west of the Ganges, which comes from the north".[116]

Based on these considerations one can conceive an ideal plan of the city Pāṭaliputra that conforms equally to the account of Megasthenes and to the information in the Indian literature (Fig. 28). One may pose the question as to the extent to which this tallies with the results of archeological research in Patna.[117] The basic confirmation of the report of Megasthenes by archaeological results has been known for a long time. More than 100 years ago during the excavation of a trench, one encountered the wooden city defenses described by Megasthenes. Over time the remains of palisades were discovered in different places[118] during the course of building excavation, and in 1926/27 on one of these sites systematic excavations were carried out, which shed light on the character of the defenses. These consist of a double row of standing beams, 4.6 m high, built at intervals of 4.85 m. They are fixed by wooden cross members at the top and the bottom. Whether this defensive gangway was built on top of an earthen rampart, like the stone walls of other cities, was not determined.[119]

[116] ASIR 8, 1878, p. 28, after H.M. Elliot, *Mohammadan Historians*, Vol. IV, p. 477.

[117] ASIR 3, 1871, p. 1-34; 11, 1880, p. 151-63; 15, 1883, p. 1-3; L.A. Waddell, *Discovery of the exact site of Aśoka's classic capital or Pāṭaliputra*, Calcutta 1892; L.A. Waddell, *Report on Excavations at Pāṭaliputra*, Calcutta 1903; P.C. Mukerji, *A Report on the Excavations on the ancient site of Pāṭaliputra (Patna-Bankipur) in 1896/97*, Calcutta (not available to me); ARASI 1912/13, p. 53-86; 1913/14, p. 53ff.; 1914/15, p. 16f.; 1915/ 16, p. 27ff.; 1926/27, p. 135-40; 1935/36, p. 54-55; ASI, Progr. Rep. Eastern Circle 1912/ 13, p. 55-61; 1913/14, p. 45-74; 1914/15, p. 46-60; M. Ghosh, *Pāṭaliputra*, 1919 (not available to me); Ind. Arch. 1953/54, p. 18f.; 1955/56, p. 22f.; A.S. Altekar and V. Mishra, *Report on Kumrahar excavations* 1951-55, Hist. Res. Ser. III, Patna 1959; Patil, p. 371-421.

[118] A. S. Altekar reports (p. 6) that the remains of palisades have been found, "from Lohanipur in the west, through Bahadurpur, Bulandibagh, Kumrahar, Maharajkhand and Sewai Tank to Gandhi Tank in the east near the Chowk". On the following page the sites appear "Lohanipura, Bulandibagh, Bahadurpur, Kumrahar, Maharajakhand, Sevai Tank and Gandhi Tank". Thus on p. 14 one reads: "Remains of the Mauryan palisades were found, as already mentioned, in the Gandhi tank (formerly known as Mangle's tank) south of the Chowk, in Mahrajkhand and Tulsimandi to the north-east of Kumrahar, at Kumrahar and Bulandibagh and at Lohanipur and at many other places." One would be curious to know which other sites might be meant. In the map appended to the publication only three sites are given, namely Bulandibagh, Mahrajkhand and Gandhi Tank; the same holds for the map of Waddell. Except for Bulandibagh (see the following note) and Gandhi Tank (see p. 42 note 142), only two further sites are mentioned in the excavation reports: first Lohanipur, "remains of a wooden palisade with the wooden drain at its bottom" (P.C. Mukherji, loc. cit. 232ff.) and second, Mahrajkhand, "a cluster of about twenty-five to thirty beams ... *sal* tree" (Waddell, p. 22).

[119] ARASI 1926/27, p. 137: "It seems to have been a wide wooden wall, hol-

If one joins together the different points in which the remains of this fortification have been found, one observes surprisingly that a nearly straight line of over 8 km length is preserved. This confirms archaeologically more than half of the length that Megasthenes gives for the city defenses. There can be little doubt that we are dealing here with the southern border of the city. The building of a city is only sensible on the northern higher ground, which is not as threatened by flooding, and only here could medieval and modern Patna develop. Up to the present day, the area to the south of this line the area is frequently flooded and thus not suited for building.[120]

The southern border of the city is thus established, and we can now turn to the eastern edge, that is, the short side of the parallelogram to the right. Scholarly suggestions on this matter have been mere guesses, while an unnoticed remark in an old excavation report provides the key to understanding it. According to the report, in 1876 in a place named Sheikh Mithia Ghari in Patna, workers dug a trench approximately between the market and railway station. They encountered a brick wall that ran from the northwest to the southeast, in addition to the palisade defenses mentioned by Megasthenes, which ran nearly parallel a short distance away from this wall.[121] Contrary to the other exca-

low inside to serve possibly as a passage ... The width of the palisade across the wooden uprights is about 14´-6", and these uprights were spanned originally at the top by beams." Cf. R.E.M. Wheeler, AI 4, 1947/48, p. 96: "A double line of upright timbers, 15 feet high, 14 ½ feet between the parallel lines, and bounded together by a 'floor' and a 'roof' of cross-timbers, has been traced for a considerable distance and appeared to the excavator to 'extend almost indefinitely'. Whether this was a passage within an earthen rampart or whether, as is more likely, the structure was filled with earth and formed its core or revetment, was not ascertained, although the point is one which could readily be determined by trained observation."

[120] Cf. P.P. Karan, *Patna and Jamshedpur,* GRI 14, 1952, p. 27: "The axis of the city lies parallel to the Ganges, which is characterised by a high bluff rising immediately above the stream, which is not liable to inundation even in the years of high flood. The low lying area to the south of Patna is liable to flooding every year by the Punpun and the Phalgu rivers which are typical hill streams in the south, where their shallow beds are suddenly overflooded after a heavy rainfall in the Chota Nagpur highland. The level on which Patna is situated, which forms an obstacle to the natural flooding is due to the natural drainage of the streams from the south and forces the water to flow parallel to the Ganges until it joins the latter east of Luckeesarai. The extension of the city to the south is, therefore, restricted by the possibility of inundation."

[121] J.W. McCrindle, *Ancient India as described by Megasthenes,* p. 207; Waddell, p. 21: "...1876 while digging a tank in Sheikh Mithia Ghari, a part of Patna almost equally distant from the Chauk (market-place) and the railway-station...a long brick wall from NW-SE...Not far from the wall and almost parallel to it was found a line of Palisades."

vation contexts, the defenses thus ran not in an east-west direction but rather from northwest to southeast! In this place we can only be dealing with the eastern edge of the city. The direction conforms to that of Megasthenes's city parallelogram (Fig. 29).

Thus, the western border of old Pāṭaliputra has to be sought some kilometers west of present-day Patna, and the northern demarcation had approximately the same position as the current bank of the Ganges. One must, however, take into consideration the fact that the northern palisade and perhaps also the northernmost part of the city have been eroded away by the Ganges.[122] Certainly, the Ganges destroyed all of the places that the Chinese pilgrim to India, Hiuen-Tsiang,[123] described as lying north of the city: the stone column, Aśokas "hell" (a small town with about 1000 houses on the bank of the Ganges), the stūpa with Vihāra, an Aśoka column about 9 m high, and, finally, Mahendra's mountain and the hollowed out stone. Had one taken Megasthenes's data regarding size and form into consideration, one would have saved oneself the trouble of seeking these monuments.[124]

But the situation is different with regard to the monuments that Hiuen-Tsiang found south of the old city. He reports a ruined tower, a hill in the southwest, and further to the southwest a ruin comprising five stūpas that resembled five hills.[125] These monuments can be confidently identified with the "five hills" (Panc Pahadi)[126] that lie 2 km south of Patna. Together with the Chota Pahadi hills to their north, these represent the only landscaping in the plain south of Patna. But this identification still requires archaeological confirmation. The excavations carried out by Cunningham, Führer, and Spooner lead one to believe that we are in fact dealing with stūpas.[127]

[122] F. Buchanan observed in 1812, "where the river washes away the bank many old walls are laid open"; cf. F. Buchanan, *Journal kept during the survey of the districts of Patna and Gaya,* ed. by V.H. Jackson, Patna 1925; cited by Patil, p. 406.

[123] Beal, Vol. II, p. 85ff.

[124] The study of L.A. Waddell, *Discovery of the exact site of Aśoka's classic capital of Pāṭaliputra,* Calcutta 1892, consists mostly of these kinds of attempts at identification.

[125] Beal, Vol. II, p. 94: "To the south-west of the mountain is a collection of five stūpas. The foundations are lofty but ruinous; what remains, however, is a good height. At a distance they look like little hills."

[126] D.R. Patil, *The Antiquarian Remains in Bihar,* Patna 1963, p. 381: "a range of mounds or hillocks covering an area 8000´ x 600´ They stand out prominently in the otherwise low-level plain most of which is under water in the rainy season. ... The group of the hillocks is populary called Pancha Pahadi, i.e. five hills, but the mounds are actually only two in number at present." The identification can be found in Waddell, p. 52ff.

[127] Cf. Patil, p. 382.

The plan of Pāṭaliputra reconstructed after Megasthenes sheds new light on the archaeological contexts in Patna. As revealed by stray finds, old Patna lies buried 6-8 m below Patna's present-day surface. Only one ancient ruin worth mention is exposed on the surface of the city. A hill known as Bhikna Pahadi, about 6 m high,[128] in the western part of Patna about 800 m south of Patna College. Excavations in the late 19th century brought to light a brick building; however, little was recognizable with regard to either its structure or its significance.[129] Waddell connects this monument with a legend handed down by pilgrims to India. At the command of Aśoka the gods erected an artificial mountain of stone blocks around the cave in which his brother meditated, which was to be a hermitage in the city for him.[130] In order to recognize the real meaning of this brick building, we must turn to the Arthaśāstra, according to which temples to the gods are to be built in the center of a city.[131] Temples of this kind, in fact, can be identified in some of the relevant cities.[132] Most of these buildings are relatively late in date. It became evident in some cases, however, that they were built on the foundations of older sanctuaries. When we move from the known borders of old Pāṭaliputra and identify the center of the parallelogram,

[128] Waddell, p. 13: "This 'hill' I found to be an artificial mound about 20 feet high and about a quarter of a mile in circuit, consisting apparently of brick ruins, not stone." In his report of 1892, *Discovery of the exact site of Aśoka's classic capital or Pāṭaliputra*, on the other hand Waddell gives the height of the hill as 40´ and the circumference as one mile (p. 7).

[129] Patil, p. 385: "Part of the mound was excavated in 1897 by P.C. Mukerji who exposed only brick rubble and debris of ancient buildings with finds of only a carved brick, a terra-cotta figure and a crystal. No Buddhist antiquity as such has been reported from the mound."

[130] Fa-hsien, Giles, 45; Hiuen-Tsiang, Beal, p. 91ff.

[131] KA. 2,4,17; *Aparājit Āpratihata Jayanta Vaijayanta Koṣṭhān Śiva Śvaiśravaṇ Āśvi Śrī Madirāgṛhāṇi ca pura-madhye kārayet*, "in the middle of the city he has to be made shrines for Aparājita, Apratihata, Jayanta and Vaijayanta, as well as houses of Śiva, of Vaiśravaṇa, of the Aśvins, of Śrī and of Madirā".

[132] Bhita, ASIR 3, p. 51: "a single mound standing in the midst of the hollow, This was most probably the site of a temple"; ARASI 1911/12, p. 40: "The building 50 is a temple of late Gupta Times which was partially excavated by Dr. Führer some years ago"; (old) Rājagṛha, Patil, p. 441ff.: "The Maṇiyār Maṭh..., situated almost in the centre of the enclosure of the inner city" (this monument was originally probably of a temple devoted to snake worship which was rebuilt and added onto several times); Kauśāmbī, ASIR 10, p. 1: "the Jain temple, which is the highest point in the old city, and which I have little doubt that it was the site of the Buddhist temple which enshrined the famous sandalwood statue of the Great Teacher", Sisupalgarh, AI 5, p. 78: "Towards the centre of the fort can be seen a group of sixteen monolithic pillars,... no digging was done in this area, but it looks as though a pillared hall stood here once."

it becomes clear that this center falls exactly on the spot of the Bhikna Pahadi monument. It remains open to which deity this sanctuary in the middle of the city was dedicated.[133] According to the theory of the Arthaśāstra, north of the city center was the royal residence.[134] Applying this to Pāṭaliputra would mean that the castle of the Maurya rulers north of Bhikna Pahadi could be sought in the area of the present-day university campus. As long as no excavations have taken place in this area with such considerations, we depart the realm of that which is provable.[135]

The search for the famous palace and government buildings[136] of the Maurya rulers was one of the main goals of archaeological research in Patna. For some time, people also believed they had discovered a considerable part of this palace and thereby to have fixed its location. In the early 20th century, D.B. Spooner discovered the remains of a columned hall in Kumrahar, a place which lies ½ km southeast of the excavated palisade defenses located

[133] According to a legend handed down by Hemacandra (ed. Bibl. Ind., N.S. 66, p. 190f.) about the founding of Pāṭaliputra, in the center of the city a sanctuary of Jina was built: *purasya tasya madhye tu jināyatanam utttamam nṛpatiḥ kārayām asa śāśvatāyatanopamam ||181||*, "but in the center of this city the king had an elevated site of Jina be erected comparable to a non ephemeral site". One can hardly attribute historical value to this legend of the founding of the city, not to mention the other similar legends. It is governed by the tendency to bring a noted sanctuary into the context of one's own cult.

[134] KA. 2,4,7: *vāstu-hṛdayād uttare nava-bhāge yathokta-vidhānam antaḥpuraṃ prāṇmukham udaṅ-mukhaṃ vā kārayet,* "Seen from the center of the building site, in the northern ninth building sector in the order just mentioned (the king) has to be made his royal residence built with the foremost front toward the east or north." In the regulation for the laying out of a field camp, which is reproduced in all details of the city description, correspondingly one learns from KA. 10,1,2: *madhyamasyottare nava-bhāge rāja-vāstukaṃ dhanuḥ-śatāyāmam ardha-vistāraṃ, paścimārdhe tasyāntaḥpuram,* "In thenorthern ninth building sector — as viewed from the center point — is the king's ground 100 bows long and half as wide, in the western half of which, the royal residence (is located)."

[135] The considerable difference in size between the 64 gate Pāṭaliputra and the 12 gate normal city of the Arthaśāstra makes the use of its directive on the position of the royal residence somewhat questionable with regard to Pāṭaliputra. Moreover, it seems that the north definition used in the Arthaśāstra — probably defined by cultic grounds — does not seem to make the north obligatory. In two passages it is emphasized that the king's palace should lay in a terrain suitable for building: KA. 2,4,6: *pravire vastuni,* "on splendid building terrain", KA. 1,20,1: *vāstuka-praśaste deśe,* "in an area that is recommended as a construction site".

[136] According to a saga transmitted by Fa-hsien, the king's palace should have been built by superhuman beings. Giles, p. 45: "The king's palace in the city, with its various halls, all built by spirits who piled up stones, constructed walls and gates, carved designs, engraved and inlaid, after no human fashion, is still in existence."

in Bulandi Bagh. Further excavations in 1951-55 showed this structure to be a hall.[137] This structure, rectangular in plan, has eight rows of 10 columns each placed at regular intervals. The columns are nearly 10 m in height, each of which was planted in the earth to a depth of 2.75 m. Strangely enough, even this non-visible part of the foundations was polished. The hall was probably accessible from the south where the foundations of an entry area and wooden platforms came to light, which probably supported a wide flight of stairs and were connected to a canal.

The first glimpse of the remains of this structure evoked speculations regarding its function. Inspired by the dependence of architectural sculpture on Achaemenid images, Spooner compared the hall with columned halls in Persepolis and also took them to be a royal audience hall.[138] Although Spooner at first expressed himself cautiously,[139] the conviction crystallized with him and his successors that they had found the seat of Mauryan government in Kumrahar.[140] The columned hall could not have stood alone, but rather must have been a part of an elaborate palace complex.[141] In light of this, excavations were undertaken in 1951-55 that resulted in disappointment. The excavators express their regret and their surprise that in the area of the hall they encountered no palace-like or administrative buildings,

[137] Altekar, p. 22ff. With regard to the earlier excavations in Kumrahar, see Patil, p. 386-391.

[138] Cf also J.J. Modi, *Ancient Pāṭaliputra, Dr. D.B. Spooners Recent Excavations at its site and the Question of the Influence of Ancient Persia upon India,* JBBRAS 24, 1916/17, p. 457-532.

[139] ARASI 1912/13, p. 80: "It is of course too early to hazard any judgement as to the identity of the pillared hall itself, or even as regards the general nature of the building. It may have been the Hall of Conference of an exceptionally vast and important monastery; it may have been the Hall of Audience, or even the Throne-room, of the Mauryan Palace. One can only guess at this stage of excavation, and guesses are unprofitable ... It would be unwise therefore, where the documents are so few, to dogmatize unduly, or to over-emphasize the exceptional nature of the Kumrahar hall. Such pillared halls may perhaps have been common after all."

[140] See for example M. Wheeler, *Early India and Pakistan: To Asoka,* New York, 1959, p. 177: "Inadequate though the evidence might be, it is tolerably clear that we have here a Persian *diwan* or *apadana* or audience hall." V. S. Agrawala, *Mauryan Art: The Mauryan Palace at Pāṭaliputra, Studies in Indian Art,* Varanasi 1965, p. 57: "There Dr. Spooner made excavations in 1912 and explored the remains of that particular portion of the Mauryan palace, which must have been its *Āsthāna-Maṇḍapa* or the hall of public audience (also called *Sabhā*)."

[141] ARASI, *Eastern Circle,* 1913/14, p. 62: "But in any case, whether we traced foreign influence in the hall or not, it seemed inevitable that it could not have stood in splendid isolation. ... The hall must then in any case have been but one member of a larger complex."

either from the Maurya or from later periods. It was only to prove the existence of a few monastic settlements and sanctuaries in the areas close to and farther from the halls.[142] But the excavators did not give up hope of finding administrative buildings in the area of Kumrahar and explain their lack of success with the comment that they had not yet found the right place.[143]

Given this, it is not difficult to understand why no governmental buildings came to light in Kumrahar and also why such could not be found. As we previously saw, Kumrahar is located ½ km southeast of the palisade defenses in Bulandi Bagh and thus outside the city borders on the country road between the city wall and the old course of the river. It is impossible that the residence of the king would have been located outside the protective city walls. Whereever royal castles find mention in the Indian literature, it is described as located within the city. That Pāṭaliputra did not form an exception to the rule is proven by the Chinese pilgrim Fa-hsien, who mentions that the castle, which was extant in his time, was located "in the city".[144] Outside the city walls one could find monastic settlements and sanctuaries[145] and also, near cooling waters, places of amusement for the court and the residents of the city. The canal, which came to light in front of the columned hall in Kumrahar, probably connected the hall with the bank of the Śoṇa river.[146] Similar, but considerably smaller, halls occur at Nagarjunakonda directly on the riverbank.[147] The

[142] Altekar, p. 15: "To our great regret and surprise we did not find the remains of any Mauryan structures anywhere in the extensive areas excavated in KR I to KR VIII. Nor did we come across any administrative buildings either of the Mauryan or of later periods ... Instead of finding administrative buildings we came across a number of monastic structures in KR I, KR II, KR IV, KR VII and KR VIII covering a period of about 750 years, from c. 150 B.C. to c. 600 A.D."

[143] Altekar, p. 16: "Administrative buildings might have existed in Kumrahar, whose extensive site extends much beyond the village of that name. These still remain to be located. We agree with Spooner in observing that 'we have not yet reached the proper part of the site'."

[144] See above p. 40 note 136.

[145] KA. 2,4,20: *bahiḥ parikhāyā dhanuḥ-śatāpakṛṣṭāś caitya-puṇyasthāna-vana-setubandhāḥ kāryāḥ, yathādiśaṃ ca dig-devatāḥ,* "one hundred bow-shot distance removed from the moat, sanctuaries are to be built, cult sites, forests, and irrigation facilities, as well as — corresponding to the respective direction — the deities of the directions".

[146] Altekar, p. 25: "It is not unlikely that this canal to the south of the Hall was first connected with a branch of the Śoṇa."

[147] IA 1955/56, p. 24: "*Site XXI* comprised pillared halls right on the river-edge with no traces of *chaitya* or *stupa* constructions. Their orientation was not helpful beyond suggesting that they were probably a place of popular assemblage near water-side"; p. 25: "*Site V-2* revealed a pillared pavilion with floors paved with stone slabs and walls of bricks. *Site V-4* comprised on the face of it

one at Pāṭaliputra corresponds to the size and richness of the city, so that a freestanding hall was built here with such impressive dimensions.

Several questions about the history of Pāṭaliputra must remain for the time unanswered. The reasons for the decline of the city in the mid first millennium CE[148] are just as unknown as are the time of and the reason for its origin. With regard to the origin of Pāṭaliputra, scholarship usually relies on the traditions of Buddhists and Jains, which date the city's foundation during the lifetime of their founders. According to a Buddhist legend, the expansion of a village named Pāṭaligrāma into the city of Pāṭaliputra was the result of a dispute that the Magadha ruler Ajātaśatru of Rājagṛha had with the Vṛjis. The minister of Ajātaśatru had the building area of the future city surveyed, a city that was to serve as a bastion against the Vṛjis. With his superhuman vision, the Buddha sees that mighty gods have occupied the building area and that mighty people will inhabit the site.[149]

Unfortunately, it is usual to divest reports of this type of their mythological elements and to take what remains to delve into without further arguments as the historical core. While it cannot be excluded that a legend contains a historic core, it is doubt-

a low mound with a pillared hall at its lower level to the east. In the pillared-hall area, at the lowest level, in the layer below that on which the pillars themselves had been erected, was discovered a memorial pillar-inscription in mixed Sanskrit-Prakrit, clearly belong ing to the early fourth century A.D. It records the erection of the pillar to recapitulate the valour of Sri Chantamula, who was a commander."

[148] During his visit in 629 CE, Hiuen-Tsiang encountered only ruins of the long decayed city, Beal, p. 86: "now there only remain the old foundation walls (of the city). The *saṅghārāmas,* Deva temples, and *stūpas* which lie in ruins may be counted by hundreds. There are only two or three remaining (*entire*)." Altekar, p. 12, explains the fall of Pāṭaliputra to a (thus far archaeologically unproven) catastrophic flood around the year 575 ACE. Without specific source information, he cites the Jaina work Titlhogālī, which was edited in 1974-75 with Sanskrit *chāyā* and Hindi translation by Kalyanavijayajī, Jalore, Vīra Saṃvat 2500. Concerning the date of this work, Dr. C.B. Tripathi informs me in a letter the following: "The work was dated by Muni Kalyanavijaya, Vīranirvāṇasaṃvat aur jainakālagaṇanā, Nāgarī Pracāriṇī 10/11, p. 98-103, to between the end of the 4th century and the beginning of the 5th century according to Vikrama. Probably it is even later for in it the destruction of the city Valabhī (today Vala on the peninsula Kathiawad) finds mention which took place 766 A.D. (cf. Dutt, *Chronology of India,* p. 67)." I thank Dr. Tripathi additionally for the reference that the account of the catastrophic flood in Pāṭaliputra also is cited in the *Vividhatīrthakalpa,* ed. Jinavijaya, Singhi Jaina Ser. 10. 1934, p. 39f. According to this report the Ganges flooded the city: *tao Gaṅgāe puraṃ samaggaṃ pi palavijjhihī,* "then the city will be entirely destroyed by the Ganges". *palavijjihī,* "then the city will be entirely destroyed by the Ganges".

[149] MPS 5,2-12 = D. II, p. 86f.

ful that it must in any case contain one. Here it seems less likely that a historic tradition gave the impetus for the legend. The tendency more probably was to explain the tremendous size of this city using the prophecy of the Buddha, and also to explain why the name Pāṭali village (*-grāma*) became Pāṭali city (*-putra*). This very point, however, weakened the credibility of the legend, for the second part of the city's name, *putra* ("son"), can hardly be accepted as meaning "city".[150] Thus the name of the village from which the city is to have arisen reveals itself as false and thus ahistorical.

Later times spun further legends that explain the city's name. One such story relates that the name arises from the combination of the personal names of the married couple who founded the city, a princess Pāṭalī and a prince Putraka.[151] According to another story, a student is to have married the daughter of the deity of a Pāṭali tree. The son (*putra*) born to them was thus Pāṭali-*putra* after whom the city was named.[152] The fact that the city's name cannot be explained satisfactorily[153] is an argument that demonstrates its great age. Moreover, the antique nature of the city defenses also is evident. Pāṭaliputra is the only old Indian city with a wooden wall. All other cities that have been researched, as we have seen, have a wall of stone or brick atop the rampart. Since in India wooden buildings preceded those with stone, a wooden wall is undoubtedly older than a stone one. The

[150] PW IV, p. 631: "Wilson in the introduction to Dacak. p. 7 is of the opinion that *Pāṭaliputra* is only a corruption of *Pāṭalipura* (cf. *kusumapura, puṣpapura*). We cannot agree with this since the transition of the so well known and in this context so readily understandable *pura* into *putra* is not compelling" (translated).

[151] Kathās. I, 3.

[152] Beal, p. 83ff.

[153] Cf. M. Mayrhofer, *Kurzgefaßtes etymologisches Wörterbuch des Altindischen* II, p. 246: "Unclear place-name. The anterior part could very well be *pāṭali-* ‚Stereospermum suaveolens' (see *patālaḥ*). -putra-, on the other hand, is probably a popular etymology (and hypersanskrit?), altered for a mi. or foreign expression" (translated). None of the attempted derivations that Mayrhofer cites (*-puṭa* "pocket, fold"; * *-pūrta* "Furt"; dravid. *putro*) sounds satisfactory. Also the derivation of the anterior part is highly dubious, since we probably are not deriving from Sanskrit *pāṭali*, but rather from Prakrit **pāliṃ*; cf. L. Petech, *Northern India according to the Shui-Ching-Chu*, 42: "I may point out that Pa-lien-fu (ancient paliän-piuət) transcribes the same Prakrit form *Pāliṃput(ra) which appears in Megasthenes as Palimbothra." According to A.S. Altekar, p. 3, Pāṭali trees do not occur in the area of Pāṭaliputra: "Pāṭali is no doubt the name of a species of trees, called Flueggea Leucopyrus in Latin; but according to Professor B.P. Roy, the Head of the Botany Department of Patna University, this species is found in Burma, the Punjab and the Deccan peninsula from Canara southwards. It is quite abundant in Ceylon, but not known to Bihar. Other sub-species of the shrub grow in eastern Bihar, but not in or around Patna."

old name for wooden defenses, *sāla* ("Sal wood"), later came to designate walls in general[154] and completely lost its meaning with regard to the building material, wood. In this way the author of the Arthaśāstra,[155] who forbids the use of wooden fortifications in view of their combustibility, uses the expression *sāla* unhesitatingly for the stone walls.[156] If Pāṭaliputra had a wooden wall at a time when other cities for some time had ones of stone, this suggests that those defenses derive from a very old period. A simple C14 assay might shed light on the age of the palisades of Pāṭaliputra and therewith contribute to the solution of the question of the origin of this, the largest city of antiquity.

As far as known, the majority of the Indo-Āryan cities were founded in the first half of the first pre-Christian millennium. Their origin falls thus in the same time as that of the Greek cities.[157] In their creation, moreover, both city cultures show several similarities. The regular layout of a system of parallel streets that cross at right angles, a system that came to the fore in 5th-century Greece, followed a time of planless buildings,[158] a process that is also documented in India. Despite this city planning, the Indian

[154] Rām. 6,39,20: *purī... kāñcanena ca śālena*, "the city... with a golden wall"; Rām. 1,5,12: *sāla-mekhalām*, "the wall encircled (city)" Kum. 6,38: *Gaṅgā-srotaḥ-parikṣiptaṃ vaprāntara-jvalitauṣadhi... maṇi-śilā-sālaṃ*, "with the Ganges flowing around, with shining plants on the city wall, with a wall of precious stone blocks". See Ch. 2. p. 58 note 1.

[155] KA. 13,4,9: *parikṣipya durgaṃ khāta-sālābhyāṃ*, "the fortification along the trench and wall having been encircled (during the siege)" KA. 12,5,17: *anu-sālaṃ*, Kangle: "along the rampart" (also means *anu-śāleṣu* KA. 2,4,16 "along the walls" and not, as Kangle translates, "in enclosures"). In the description of the army camp (*skandhāvāra*) KA. 10,1,1, which imitates the description of the city, one can doubt whether *-sāla-* in the composite *khāta-vapra-sāla-dvārāṭṭālaka-saṃpannaṃ* ("provided with moat, rampart, *sāla*, gates and towers") means a wall or palisade. The usual term otherwise used for the city wall, *prākāra*, is also used for the "wood" wall of Pāṭaliputra; cf. Mahābhāṣya II, p. 311: *īdṛśā asya prākārā iti*, "such are its (i.e., Pāṭaliputra's) walls"; II, 311: *Pāṭaliputrakāḥ prākarā iti*, "the walls of Pāṭaliputra".

[156] KA. 2,3,8-9: *na tv eva kāṣṭha-mayam, agnir avahito hi tasmin vasati*, "but not made of wood, for fire lies hidden therein. "

[157] According to F. Tritsch, *Die Stadtbildungen des Altertums und die griechische Polis*, Klio 22, Leipzig 1929, the founding of Greek cities is related to the incipient contacts with the Orient during the same period: "It is not accidental that the first traces of Hellenic Greek cities occur only in the 8th and 7th century, at just the time of the beginning of contact with the East, of the first appearance of Greek script, of the earliest large stone statues and temples. Certainly, the greater stimulus for urban organization, for the formation of the *polis* which the Greeks had been completely lacking from 1100 to 800, came out of the newly developing relations with the Orient, new impressions, and the resulting expansion of their horizon, a sense for the world" (p. 62; translated).

[158] Cf. A. v. Gerkan, *Griechische Städteanlagen, Untersuchungen zur Entwicklung des Städtebaus im Altertum*, Berlin 1924, p. 28ff.

technique of city building takes a step backward as opposed to the preceding urban cultures of ancient Near Eastern and Indus cities. In a special way, the lack of a systematic sewer network gives the impression of primitiveness in Greek and Indian cities. Irregular open gutters[159] sufficed in Greece, and in India drainage pits.[160]

Since the Indian cities were located mostly in plains, here even a smoothly functioning source of fresh water as in Greece was not possible. The water was fetched from wells or from the river in front of the city gates.

Certainly, analogies in the design of Greek and Indian cities must not belie the fact that the geographically determined difference in the location of the cities involved structural differences that would lead the social and cultural developments of Greece and India in very different directions. In Greece it is not, as in India, the plains of great rivers that conditioned urban development, but rather the mountains.[161] These mountain heights were the seats of lords and retreats for settlements that arose on the slopes. When these settlements became independent of the rule of the tyrants in the castle on top of the mountain, they developed their own defenses. The military value of these walls was negligible. Decisions were sought in open battles and not in siege wars.

On the other hand, the old Indian city lay in the plain, on a river bank, favorable for traffic but accessible to all attackers. Hence it had to be protected by an elaborate defensive system of moat, rampart, and wall. The earthen rampart is without parallel in the fortifications of the ancient Orient and the Greco-Roman

[159] v. Gerkan, p. 87f.

[160] In nearly all excavations "ring-wells" occurred, which consist of a row of ceramic rings or jars with floors, without, however, any water pipes or gutters. Whether one can conclude from the mention by Megasthenes (Strabo XV,702) that the city moat served, among other purposes, to drain sewage water from the city on a planned urban drainage syste is questionable. It was probably a system to drain the rain water. Such a drain, which penetrated the palisade, was recorded in the excavations in Bulandi Bagh, cf. ARASI 1926/27, p. 138: "Another discovery of much interest was a large wooden drain contemporary with the palisade, which it crosses at right angles ... The drain measures some 40 feet in length, and it is set across the palisade so as to project equidistantly on either side of it."

[161] Cf. E. Kirsten, *Die griechische Polis als historisch-geographisches Problem des Mittelmeerraumes*, Colloquium Geographicum, Bd. 5, Bonn 1956, p. 43: "A survey of the settlement sites of the Greek mainland shows that the choice of controlling hills, of fortress hills for settlement and of the fortresses built upon them, introduced the type of settlement characteristic of the early Greeks, that is, the tribes of Ionians and Achaeans that settled Greece in the 2nd millennium" (translated).

world. It is comparable to the prehistoric and early historic circular ramparts in the Nordic areas. As opposed to these, the Indian city defenses are never circular in form. Although the form of the city is left open in the directives of the Arthaśāstra,[162] a squarish nearly quadratic form seems to have been preferred.

Different from the Greek wall, the Indian defensive system is not a secondary element but rather the constituent attribute of the city. Hence the Arthaśāstra first treats the building of the fortifications, then the planning of the city center, and the most important building, the residence of the king. Here there is a difference of great important in contrast to the Greek city. In Greece the lord of the castle in his acropolis was foreign to the city population. Once this tyrant was eliminated, a free citizenry and a democratic system of government could develop. On the contrary, in India the royal residence was located within the city. It forms the military, economic, administrative, and cultural center. The royal residence is designated with an old name the "interior city" (*antaḥpura*) and is described as being just as fortified as the city itself.[163] There are even expressions where the palace wall is confused with the city wall[164] and the castle gate with the city gate.[165] Nonetheless, it would be a false conclusion were one to consider the royal residence, on the strength of this description, to be a citadel. We know from the narrative literature that it was easy to negotiate the moat and wall of the king's palace by means of a pole[166] or rope.[167] The palace wall formed a police and not a military protection. Once besiegers had breached the city wall, the city lay at their feet. There was no last stand for the palace.[168] The last resort of the king was to flee the city and attempt to have the usurper assassinated in his palace.[169] Whoever ruled the royal

[162] KA. 2,3,3: *vṛttaṃ dīrghaṃ catur-aśraṃ vā, vāstu-vaśena vā* "round, rectangular, quadratic, or in accordance with the building ground".

[163] The fortification consisted of moat and wall without a rampart, KA. 1,20,1: *saprākāra-parikhā-dvāram... antaḥpuraṃ,* "The royal residence with wall, moat, and gate."

[164] Mahābhāṣya II, p. 342: *prāsādo Devadattasya prākāro nagarasyeti,* "the palace of Devadatta — the city wall".

[165] Jāt. II,218: *nagara-dvāra-samīpaṃ gantvā dvāra-koṭṭhakaṃ disvā idaṃ rañño vasana-gehan ti pucchitvā,* "he came to the city gate, saw the entry hall and asked: is this the dwelling of the king?"

[166] Daś. 150: *veṇu-yaṣṭim ādāya tayā śāyitayā ca parikhāṃ sthāpitayā ca prākāra-bhittim alanghayam,* "I overcame the moat by laying a bamboo pole over it, and the wall by laying it against it."

[167] Avim. P. *etad rāja-kulam aho sthiratvam ucchritatvaṃ prākārasya... iha sthitvā rajjuṃ prakṣipāmi,* "This is the house of the king. What a strength and height the wall has! ... Standing here, I want to throw a rope up."

[168] Cf. KA. 13,4,25ff.

[169] Cf. KA. 12,5,43ff.

residence, also ruled the city. A tyrannocide might well eliminate an unpopular king, but certainly never kingship per se,[170] for the structure of the city with a palace as its entre of power prevented the development of a communal form independent of kingship. Thus the fate of the city and its inhabitants lay in the hand of the king, and the fate of the king in the hand of the citizens. Different from the tyrant in his acropolis, the king could defend himself only with his citizens, never against them. As strong as a fortification might be, if things got serious all of the city inhabitants must defend themselves and stand behind their king. Even a small group of partisans of the enemy in the city could compromise the most mighty fortification. In the Arthaśāstra, the skillfully worked out psychological warfare was intended to drive a wedge between the hostile king and his subjects.[171] This is equally as understandable as the constant vying for the favor of the population, which threads its way through the directives of the Arthaśāstra. Inasmuch as the power and existence of the king hung on the favor of his subjects, the king was forced in all of his dealings to consider their welfare.

[170] Accounts of the murder of tyrants in the narrative literature are assembled in W. Ruben, *Fighting against Despots in Old Indian Literature*, ABORI XLVIII-XLIX, 1968, p. 111-118. Ruben notes that in India, as opposed to Greece, despite this antidespotism, democracy failed to develop not for material reasons but rather as a result of differing ways of thinking: "This ancient Indian way of thinking was different from that of the contemporary Greeks who replaced kingdom and tyranny... in some of their town-states like Athens by democracy" (p. 117).

[171] KA. 12,1ff.

Overview

Sanskrit name	*Modern name*	*Surface in km²*	*Circumference in km*	*Approximate form*	*Number of gates*	*Location*
Pāṭaliputra	Patna	25.50	33.8	parallelogram	64	confluence [Son]-Ganges
Kauśāmbī	Kosam	2.29	6.1	trapezoid	6	left bank of Jumna
Śrughna	Sugh	1.97	6.4	triangle	?	right bank of [Jumna]
(old-)Rājagṛha	Rajgir	1.87	6.2	trapezoid	?	valley floor
Vidiśā	Besnagar	1.72	5.4	rectangular	?	confluence Bes-Betva
Ahicchatra	Ramnagar	1.52	5.4	triangle	?	
Śrāvastī	Maheth	1.45	5.4	triangle	?	right bank of [Rapti]
Puṇḍravardhana	Mahasthangarh	1.37	4.5	rectangular	8?	right bank of Karatoya
Kaliṅganagara (?)	Sisupalgarh	1.36	4.7	square	8	right bank of Bhargaui
Ujjayinī	Ujjain	0.875	3.8	pentagon	8	right bank of Śiprā
Kānyakubja	Kanauj	0.69	3.4	triangle	?	right bank of Kālīnādī
?	Balirajgarh	0.45	2.7	trapezoid	4?	
Vijayapurī	Nagarjunakonda	0.42	2.6	trapezoid	2	right bank of Kistna
Vichī(grāma)	Bhita	0.26	2.1	square	?	south of the Jumna
(New)Rājagṛha	Rajgir	0.25	2.1	square	?	before gates of (old-)R.
?	Nandangarh	0.20	1.8	square	?	
Airikina	Eran	0.18	1.7	ellipse	?	left bank of Bina
Vaiśālī	Basarh	0.14	1.5	rectangular	4?	

The drawings are based on the following publications:

Fig. 1. ASIR 1, 1871, p. XLVIII; G.R. Sharma, *The Excavations at Kausambi*, p. 5 (aerial photo).
Fig. 2. ASIR 2, 1871, p. LXXI.
Fig. 3. ARASI 1913/14, p. LXXI; AI 7, 1951, 67, Fig. 1.
Fig. 4. ASIR 10, 1880, pl. XII.
Fig. 5. ASIR 1, 1871, pl. XLIII.
Fig. 6. ARASI 1907/08, pl. XXII.
Fig. 7. ASIR 15, 1883, pl. XXIX.
Fig. 8. AI 5, 1949, Fig. 1 and p. XXVII (aerial photo).
Fig. 9. Ind. Arch. 1956/57, 21.
Fig. 10. ASIR 1, 1871, pl. XLVII.
Fig. 11. Ind. Arch. 1962/63, Fig. 1.
Fig. 12. Ind. Arch. 1957/58, Fig. 4; Ind. Arch. 1958/59, Fig. 4.
Fig. 13. ASIR 8, 1873, pl. XVII; ARASI 1911/12, pl. XX.
Fig. 14. ASIR 1, 1871, p1. XXIII; ARASI 1906/07, p1. XXXVIII.
Fig. 15. ASIR X, p1. XXIII.
Fig. 16. ASIR 1, 1871, pl. XXI; *Vaiśālī Excavations*, Fig. 1.
Figs. 17-18. J. Marshall, *Taxila III*, pl. 2.
Figs. 19-20. ARASI 1911/12, pl. XII.
Figs. 21-22. ARASI 1911/12, pl. XIII.
Fig. 23. ARASI 1905/06, pl. XXXVI.
Fig. 24. Bharhut, pl. XLII.
Fig. 25. Ajanta 3, pl. XVI.
Fig. 26. Bharhut, pl. XXX,4.
Fig. 27. Bharhut, pl. XVI.
Fig. 28. (After Megasthenes and Mahābhāṣya.)
Fig. 29. Altekar, Map; Waddell, Map; USAF Pilotage Chart PC-H-9C. Fortified.

Plans of Cities

I.	Figs. 1-16 Outlines of Cities
II.	Figs. 17-19 Residential Areas and Streets
III.	Figs. 21-27 Dwellings
IV.	Figs. 28-29 Pāṭaliputra (Patna)

I. Cities

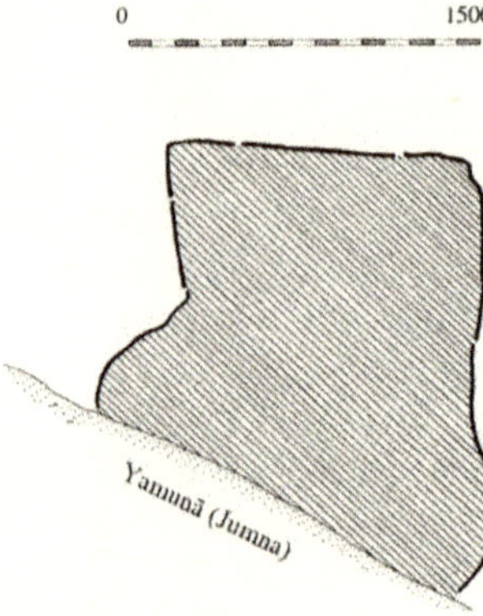

Kauśāmbī (Kosam)
Fig. 1 (p. 18f.)

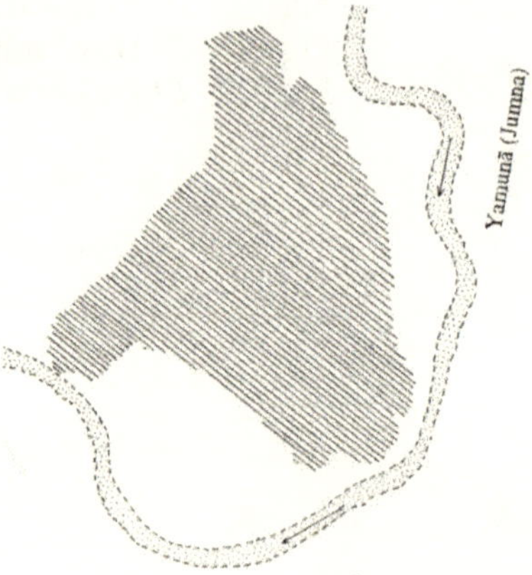

Śrughna (Sugh)
Fig. 2 (p. 18f.)

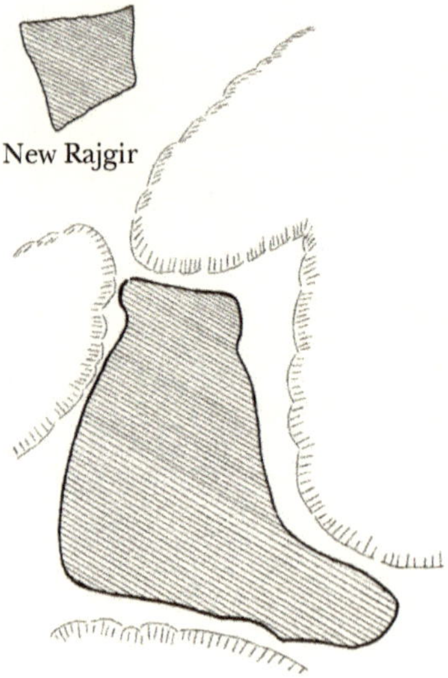

Rājagṛha (Rajgir)
Fig. 3 (p. 19)

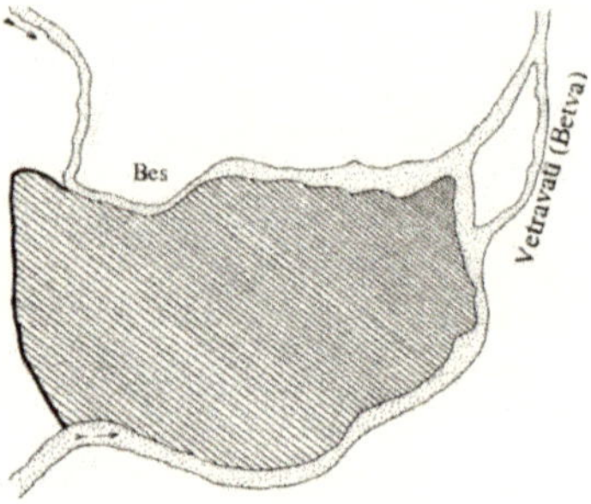

Vidiśā (Besnagar)
Fig. 4 (p. 19f.)

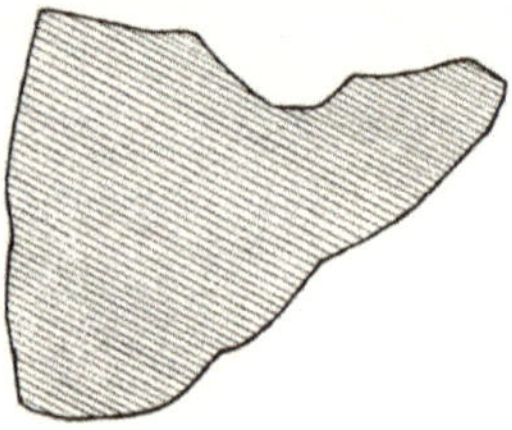

Ahicchatra (Ramnagar)
Fig. 5 (p. 20)

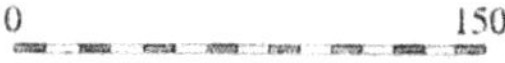

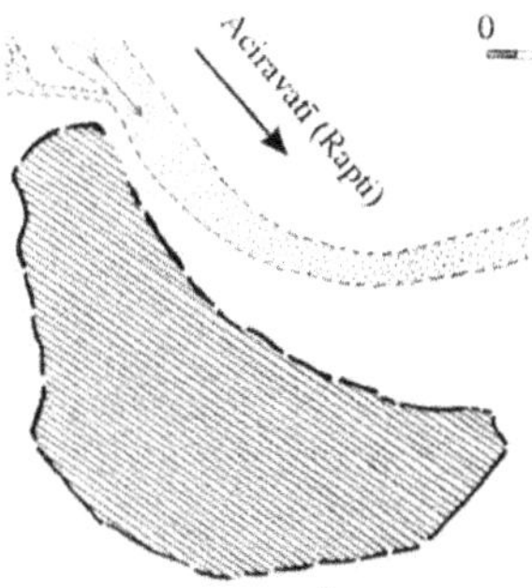

Śrāvastī (Maheth)
Fig. 6 (p. 20f.)

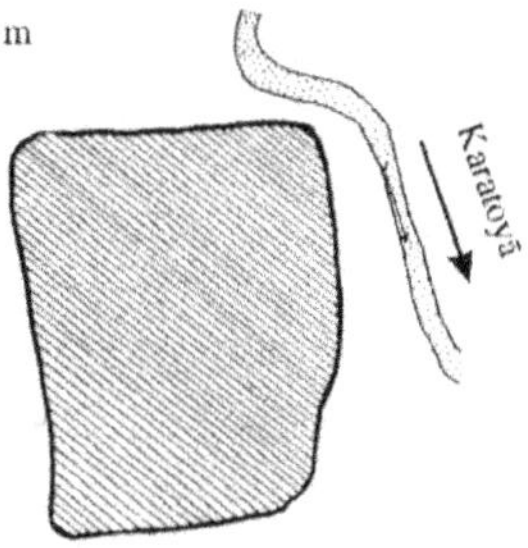

Puṇḍravardhana
(Mahasthangarh)
Fig. 7 (p. 21)

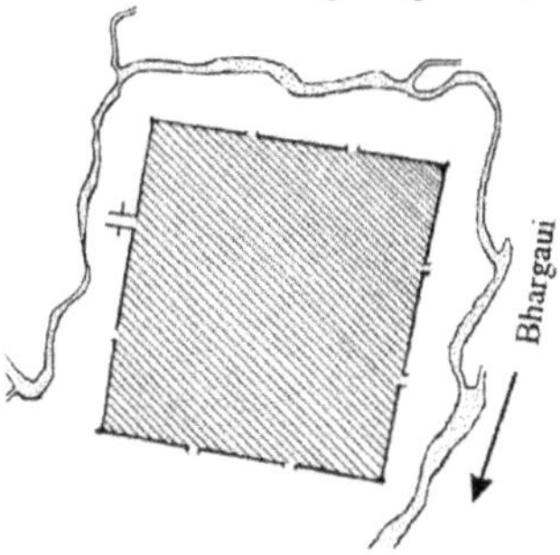

Kaliṅganagara (?) (Sisupalgarh)
Fig. 8 (p. 21)

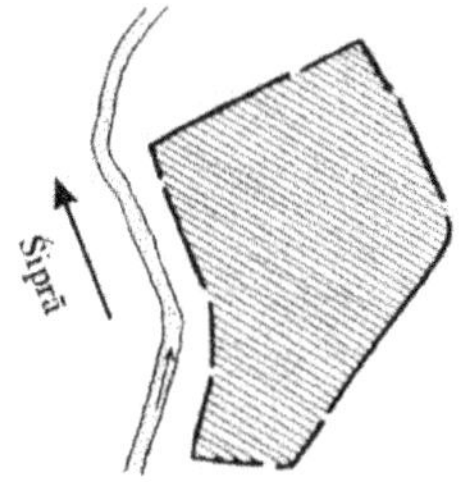

Ujjayinī (Ujjain)
Fig. 9 (p. 22f.)

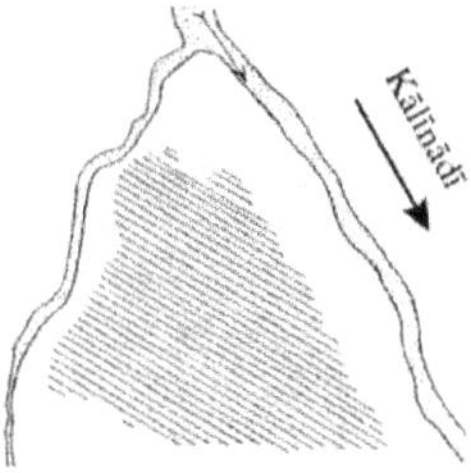

Kānyakubja (Kanauj)
Fig. 10 (p. 22)

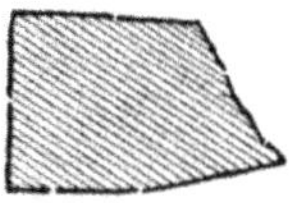

(Balirajgarh)
Fig. 11 (p. 22)

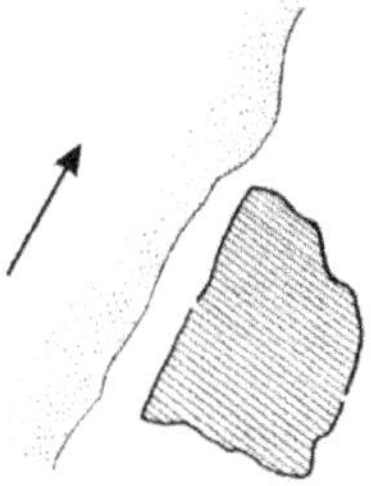

Vijayapurī
(Nagarjunakonda)
Fig. 12 (p. 22f.)

Vichī (Bhita)
Fig. 13 (p. 23)

(Nandangarh)
Fig. 14 (p. 23)

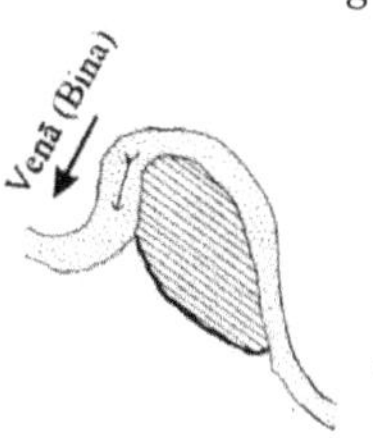

Airikina (Eran)
Fig. 15 (p. 23)

Vaiśālī (Basarh)
Fig. 16 (p. 24)

II. Residential Areas and Streets

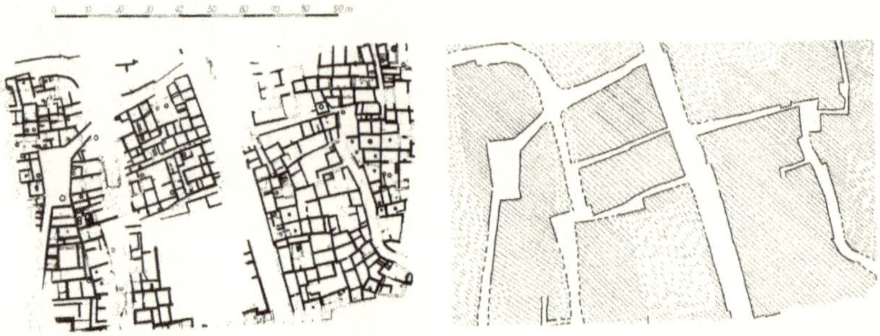

Fig. 17/Fig. 18 Taxila Bhir Mound (p. 27f.)

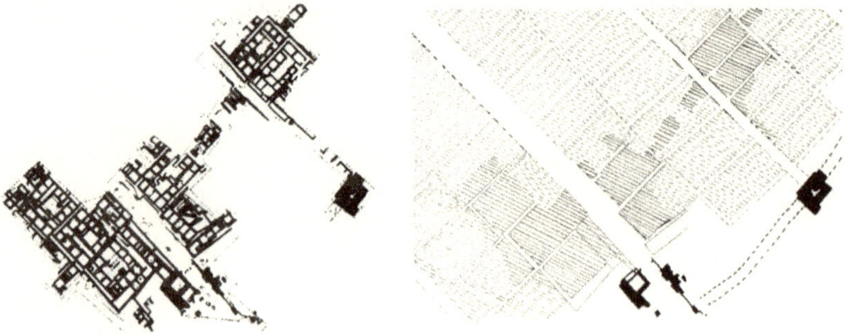

Fig. 19/Fig. 20 Bhita (p. 28)

III. Dwellings

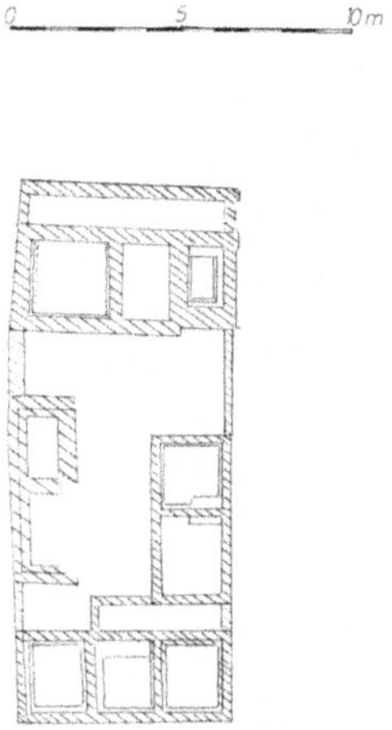

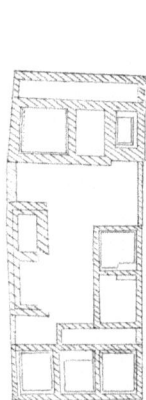

Fig. 21 House on the Bastion Street in Bhita (p. 28)

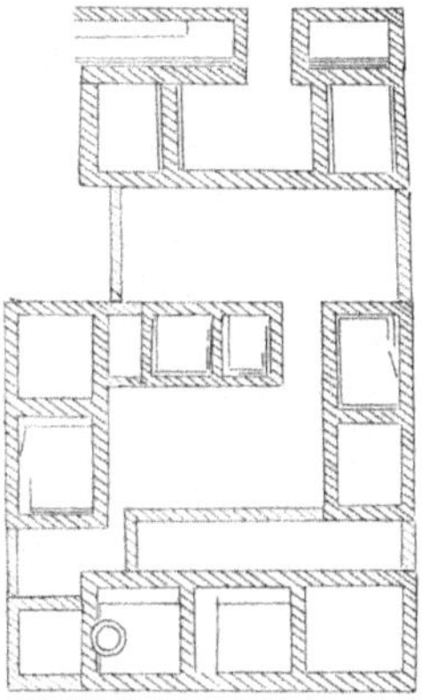

Fig. 22 House on the High Street in Bhita (p. 28)

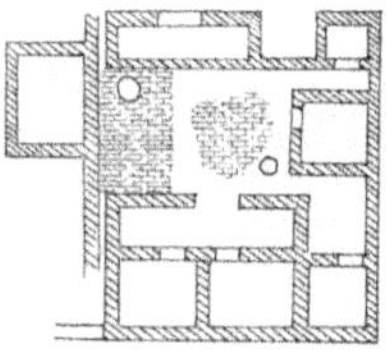

Fig. 23 House in Rājagṛha (p. 28)

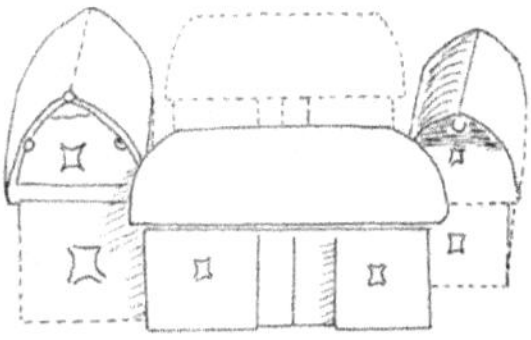

Fig. 24 Farmstead, Bharhut (p. 28f.)

Fig. 26 Facade of a two-story house, Bharhut (p. 30)

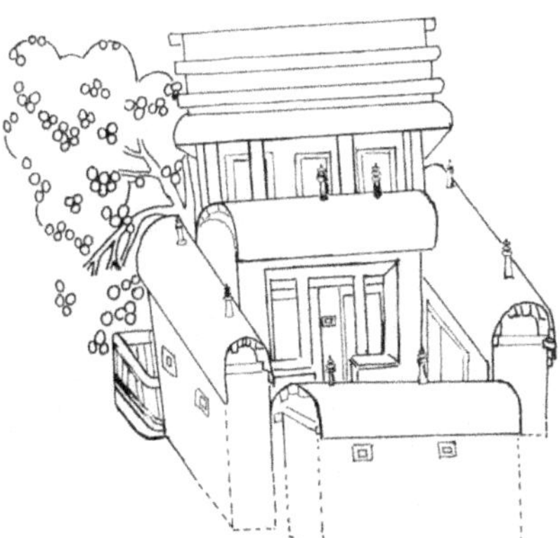

Fig. 25 Villa with entry hall and tree garden, Ajanta (p. 29)

Fig. 27 Facade of a three-story house, Bharhut (p. 30)

IV. Pāṭaliputra (Patna)

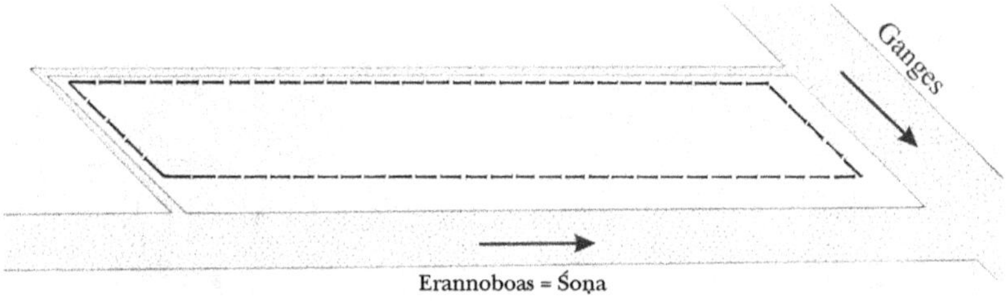

Fig. 28 Ideal plan of Pāṭaliputra
after Megasthenes and Mahābhāṣya (p. 36f.)

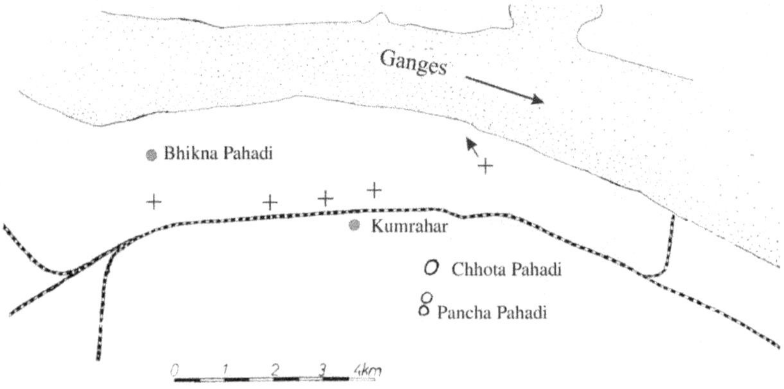

Fig. 29 Archaeological sites and palisade (+) in Patna
(the railway serves for the orientation) (p. 38)

Chapter 2

The Construction of a Fortification[*]

The wealth of factual information that the second book of the Kauṭilīya, named the activity of the Heads of Departments (*adhyakṣapracāra*), contains confronts every interpreter with the basic issue regarding its veracity. Is it a compilation of facts derived from practical experience and assembled for carrying out normal duties, or only a collection of theories bred in ethereal scholarly retreats and without contact with the realities of life? It has been commonly believed that these issues could be resolved by solving the question whether the author was a great statesman, who later in life surrounded by his advisors recorded the essence of his experience, or whether he was a politically insignificant ivory tower scholar, lacking real experience with the world. The character of the Kauṭilīya as a textbook and compendium precludes, however, such a simple solution. Because this work consists of heterogeneous components, arcane school wisdom is interspersed with practical experience, free speculation side by side sober information. Only a meticulous analysis of the content enables one to determine the value of the different sections.

By no means can such an analysis rely exclusively on the philological exegesis. It must try to comprehend the cultural phenomena that the text presents from multiple perspectives. In the following pages I examine the chapter regarding the building of defensive structures (KA. 2,3), considered the most difficult and obscure of the second book. In order to arrive at a conclusive interpretation of its content, such an examination requires, be-

[*] Revised and enlarged from the German *Arthaśāstra-Studien II, Die Anlage einer Festung (durgavidhana)*, in WZKSO 11, 1967, p. 44ff.

side the examination of literary sources,[1] the results especially of archaeological research.[2] Given that, in order to be effective, defensive constructions must meet both general architectural and military requirements, information from outside of India may be taken into consideration with due caution to illuminate the subjects dealt with in the Kauṭilīya[3].

The beginning of the chapter consists of a list of natural defenses (*daiva-kṛta*) that might serve as seats for provincial magistrates (*janapadarakṣa-sthāna*) or as refuges during emergencies (*āpady apasāra*). These include places that, by virtue of their position in water (*audaka*), on mountains (*pārvata*), in deserts (*dhānvana*), or in forests (*vana-durga*), are inaccessible.[4] The

[1] Fundamental for the study of the references to ancient Indian cities and urban fortifications in Pāli texts is the dissertation of Karam Tej Singh Sarao, *Urban Centres and Urbanisation as Reflected in the Pāli Vinaya and Sutta Piṭakas*, Diss. Cambridge 1989, with an exhaustive bibliography (p. 187-206) that includes also archaeological literature. For references from the epics, see J.K. de Cock, *Eene oudindische stad volgens het Epos*, Diss. Phil. Amsterdam 1899. Without knowledgemetn of this study and without a critical evaluation of the sources, Udai Narain Roy, *Fortifications of Cities in Ancient India*, IHQ 1954, p. 237-244, paints an image of Indian defensive building based on epic and Purāṇic texts. Equally superficial is the article by the same author, *Some Architectural Recommendations of Kauṭilya as Followed and Practised in Ancient India*, JBRS 49, 1963. Moti Chandra, *Architectural Data in Jain Canonical Literature*, JBBRAS 26, 1951, p. 169ff., comments on passages from Aupapātikasūtra, Rāyapaseṇiya, among others, while O. Stein discusses the parallels to our chapter from several Śilpaśāstras, *Arthaśāstra and Śilpaśāstra*, Arch. Or. 7, 1935, p. 473ff. Stein's compilation clearly shows how little value the Śilpaśāstras possess as a source for ancient Indian architecture. They only paraphrase the Kauṭilīya or its sources and thus can hardly serve as more than commentaries. On the study of A.K. Coomaraswamy, *Cities and City Gates*, see below Ch. 2, note 105.

[2] For recent studies on city fortifications, see A. Ghosh, *The City in Early Historic India*, Simla 1973 (repr. Delhi 1990); R.S. Sharma, *Urban Decay in India*, Delhi 1987; Dilip K. Chakrabarti, *The Archaeology of Ancient Indian Cities*, Delhi 1995; F.R. Allchin (ed.), *The Archaeology of Early Historic South Asia: The Emergence of Cities and States*, Cambridge 1995; M. Brandtner, *Kaliṅga und seine Hauptstadt in frühgeschichtlicher Zeit*, Hamburg 2001; P. Yule/W. Böhler, *Śiśupalgarh: An Early Historic Fortress in Coastal Orissa and its Cousins*, Beiträge zur allgemeinen und vergleichenden Archäologie, 24, 2004, p. 15-29. The following investigation is based solely on the excavation reports published in several monographs, and the Annual Reports of the Archaeological Survey of India (ARASI) and since 1946 the Bulletin of the Archaeological Survey of India as well as Indian Archaeology (Ind. Arch.).

[3] Highly instructive is Yigael Yadin's treatment of defensive architecture in the Near East in his *The Art of Warfare in Biblical Lands*, Jerusalem 1963. For a general account of ancient fortification, see P.E. Delair, *Essai sur les fortifications anciènnes*, Paris 1875; and Sidney Toy, *A History of Fortification from 300 A.D. to A.D. 1700*, London 1955. Toy deals with medieval defenses in his study *The Strongholds of India*, London 1957, and *Fortified Cities of India*, London 1966.

[4] These names rely on a list that cites six different kinds of fortifications; see Manu VII,70; Mbh. XII,87,5. For further parallels see also O. Stein, *Arthaśāstra*

passage that follows concerns itself not with the laying out of such border or refuge forts but rather with the founding and fortification of trade cities (*panya-puṭabhedana*) in the interior of the country (*janapada-madhye*). As production and market centers (*samudaya-sthānaṃ sthānīyam*),[5] these cities were dependent on facility of transportation by land and water (*aṃsapatha-vāripathābhyām*). If possible, they may be situated at the confluence of rivers (*nadī-saṃgame*) or on the sea coast. Their wealth and location with easy access resulted in these cities becoming a target of enemies and robbers out for booty. For this reason, an effective defensive system became a prime existential concern for the state and deserved a chapter of its own in an Arthaśāstra.

The instruction opens with an account of the building of moat, 4-9
rampart, and wall. Three moats (*parikhā*) were excavated;[6] they were 4
to be one staff-length (1.8 m) apart (*daṇḍāntarāḥ*) and 25.20 m, 21.60 m, and 18 m wide, respectively. Their depth should be between one half and three-fourths of their width, and the bottom width should be one third of the surface width (*tribhāga-mūla*).[7] The banks of these moats are revetted with pebbles or bricks (*pāṣāṇeṣṭakāvabaddhapārśva*).[8] They are fed by (spring)

and Śilpaśāstra, p. 479ff. In addition to the four types of forts listed in the KA., in this list the "earth fort" (*mahī-durga*) and the "man (made) fort" (Mbh. *manuṣya-durga*, Manu *nṛ-durga*), are mentioned. In Manu VII,72, the list has been grotesquely misunderstood and each of the fort types named is understood as a refuge for the relevant creatures: The 'desert fort' is a place of refuge for wild animals, the 'earth fort' for burrowing animals, the 'water fort' for aquatic animals, the 'forest fort' for birds, the 'man fort' for humans, and the 'mountain fort' for the gods.

[5] Cf. Kangle: "a *sthānīya*, the headquarters for revenue", note: "*samudayasthānam* i.e. the place where revenue is ultimately brought and kept. *sthānīyam*: this is the headquarters for 800 villages (2.1.4 above). In most cases, it is the fortified capital of the state."

[6] Descriptions of cities usually mention several moats. See, for example, Mahāvaṃsa 25,28: *nagaraṃ taṃ ti-parikhaṃ*; 25,48: *ti-mahāparikhaṃ*; Jāt. VI, p. 390; *so nagare ... udaka-parikhaṃ kaddama-parikhaṃ-sukkha-parikhan ti tisso parikhā karesi*; MPS 34,5 (p. 306): *kuśāvati rājadhānī saptabhiḥ parikhābiḥ parikṣiptā babhuva.*

[7] Meyer (translated) "Below on the ground the moat trenches are narrower so that they are less likely to collapse, as anyone knows who in his life has dug trenches." If, however, Meyer understood *tribhāga* as 'three-quarters' (Kangle correctly reads "one third"), then this incline is steep to such a degree that it hardly reduces the danger of collapse. The bottom width of one third of the upper width corresponds not only to structural statics, but also to archaeological evidence (see Fig. 8).

[8] Masonry, which strengthens the edges of trenches, occurs in ancient Ujjayinī and Kauśāmbī. For Ujjayinī, see IA 1957/58, p. 34: "During Period II (circa 500-200 B.C.), the outer edge of the moat was lined by a 3 ft. 9 in. wide brick wall. The brick lining of the succeeding Period, III, showed that during this period the width of the moat was reduced to 129 ft." G.R. Sharma, *The Excavations at Kauśāmbī* (1957-59), Allahabad 1960, p. 39: "The banks of the moat were revetted with walls built in batter."

water (*toyāntika*)[9] or are filled with water channeled into them (*āgantu-toya-pūrṇa*). This may be done, for example, from the river, in which case there must be a way for the water to drain (*parivāha*). Finally, the moats are fitted out with lotus blossoms and crocodiles (*padma- grāhavat*).[10] The earth dug out from the moat (*khātād*) is to be deposited at a distance of 7.20 m from the innermost moat (*caturdaṇḍāpakṛṣṭam parikhāyāḥ*)[11] to form a vaulted (*ūrdhva-caya*) rampart (*vapra*)[12] 10.80 m high and twice as wide. It is to have a flat back (*mañca-pṛṣṭha*) or a form like the belly of a pot (*kumbha-kukṣika*). The first of these two possibilities designates probably the usual form of a rampart, which in cross section is semi-elliptical (see Figs. 5-8), while the second brings to mind a form that corresponds to the rampart at Kauśāmbī,

[9] Kangle: "reaching down to (natural springs of) water". Differently Meyer (translated): "with water at the end (which one can let in)" and note: "The moats thus reach to a body of water." Meyer's interpretation, although linguistically possible, is unlikely, because it offers no alternative to the following *āgantu-toya*.

[10] Meyer's assumption that *padma-grāha* does not refer to lotus blossoms and crocodiles but rather to "lotus grabbers", a locking mechanism which regulates the influx of water, is unlikely. Crocodiles are mentioned at several places in the literature: Mbh. ed. Madras V, p. 1382, 3: *agādha-toyāḥ parikhā mīna-nakra-samākulāḥ*; Rām. VI,3,15 *agādhā grāhavavatyaś ca parikha mīna-sevitāḥ*; Mbh. ed. Madras XIII, p. 351, 47: *parikhās sthanu-nakra-jhasākulāḥ*; cf. Stein, *Megasthenes und Kauṭilya*, p. 376f; and *Arthaśāstra and Śilpaśāstra*, p. 481; J.K de Cock, *Eene outindische stad*, p. 25. The notion that the city moat was inhabited by crocodiles is also reflected in the oldest European travel reports, e.g., the illustrative description of the city Pegu in the *Asian Banise* of Heinrich Anselm von Zigler, ed. F. Bobertag, Berlin and Stuttgart 1883, p. 347, a description that goes back to Pinto (1509-1583): "It is built in the quadrangle and surrounded with a very strong wall pierced by four gates that face toward the east, west, south and north, respectively. This wall is surrounded by a very wide and deep moat, made dangerous by crocodiles, so that the moat bank can never be trusted... And these animals are so treacherous that when people come to fetch water with their crockery they hide beneath the reeds and then seize the poor souls by the leg or hand and drag them into the water."

[11] This distance serves to prevent the erosion of the rampart. At Ujjayinī the foot of the rampart was additionally protected from the water by means of a brick revetment: see IA 1956/57, p. 20: "The fortification on the river-side was breached by floods on at least three occasions during Period II. After the first breach, it was repaired by the construction of a 15 ft. wide brick revetment over a raised level of the rampart. This revetment, damaged during the second erosion, was available in only eleven courses of bricks. The rampart was also seen to have a brick platform, now reduced to a mass of debris, over its toe towards the moat, to prevent scouring by water."

[12] In the architectural handbooks, the unclear term *ūrdhva-caya* is paraphrased by *sotsaṅga*, *Samarāṅganasūtradhāra* 10,19 cited by Stein, *Arthaśāstra and Śilpaśāstra*, p. 482. The term *utsaṅga* (=*ucchanga, ucchaṅkha*) is to be found in the list of characteristics of a great man (see MPS 6b,8), where it characterizes the form of the Buddha's feet which, as represented in the visual arts, can be compared to a turtle. See Schlingloff, *Buddhistische Stotras*, Berlin 1955, p. 109, note 4.

the cross section of which resembles a pot turned upside down
(see Fig. 9). After elephants and cattle have tamped the earth,
the slope is planted with thorny shrubs (*kaṇṭaki-gulma*) and poisonous vines (*viṣa-vallī*).[13] On this rampart (*vaprasyopari*) should 7
be built a wall (*prākāra*) twice as wide as it is high and made of
bricks (*aiṣṭaka*)[14] (Fig. 1a), with a height between 5.40 m (*dvādaśa-
hastād*) and 10.80 m (*caturvimśati-hastād*).[15] This wall should possess an ascent for the war chariots (*rathacaryā-saṃcāra*),[16] as well
as a foundation reinforced with palmyra beams (*tāla-mūla*).[17]
The wall is to be capped with 'monkey heads', that is, with

[13] Cf. Mbh., ed. Madras V, p. 1382, 3: *khādiraiś śaṅkubhiś citāḥ.*

[14] The reliefs in Amaravati clearly show the masonry of the fortifications and the city gates, while in Sanci the gates and occasionally also the walls are rendered as smooth, which probably shows the plastering. In literature, it is mentioned several times that the walls were plastered: see, e.g., Rām. 2,80,19: *saudha-prākāra-saṃvṛtāḥ*; Vāyup. I,8,104 (p. 68): *saudhocca-vapra-prākāram.* In poetry the plastered and therefore light-colored walls on the high city ramparts are compared to the snow-capped peaks of mountains.

[15] Pāli texts give stereotypical heights of the walls as 18 hasta = 8.10 m. See Jāt. I,63,8: *aṭṭharasa-hatthubbedhaṃ pākāram*; Jāt. IV,182,10 = V,478,10: *aṭṭharas-hatthaṃ pākāraṃ.*

[16] Cf. Kangle: "evidently this passage for the movement of carts is to be on the top of the parapet, though in the case of the smaller widths, it is not easy to suppose that rathas could move freely on top". According to the preceding data regarding the width of the walls, which should comprise half of the height (2.7 m to 5.4 m), driving on top of the defenses was easily possible. Archaeological contexts show wall widths between 3 m and 7 m. In the literature the paths (carya) are mentioned several times in connection with defensive structures: see Rām. 6,75,6: *gopurāṭṭa-pratolīṣu caryāsu vividhāsu ca*; Rām. 6,59,33: *dvāreṣu caryā gṛha-gopureṣu*; Rām. 6,60,13 *caryā gopura-mūrdhasu.*

[17] Probably the reference is to beams that frame the two rows of bricks, so that the mass of the clay filling the interstices does not break apart. See Vitruvius, *Architect.* I,V,3 ed. C. Fensterbusch, Darmstadt 1964, p. 54: *Crassitudinum autem muri ita faciendam censeo, uti armati homines supra obviam venientes alius alium sine impeditione praeterire possint, dum in crassitudine perpetuae taleae oleagininieae ustilatae quam creberrime instruantur, uti utraeque muri frontes inter se, quemadmodum fibulis, his taleis conligatae aeternam habeant firmitatem*; (translated): "In my opinion, the thickness of the walls must be so built that two armed men on meeting could pass each other unhindered, while in the wider area at the ends long scorched wooden beams of olive wood as much as possible are set. In this way both frontal faces of the wall are bound together as if by bolts, having eternal strength." A similar instruction is to be found in Philon; see H. Diels and E. Schramm, *Excerpte aus Philons Mechanik BVII and VIII,* Abh. der Preussischen Akademie der Wissenschaft 1919, no. 12, p. 21 (13) (translated) "in addition, oak beams should be inserted in the walls and towers in intervals of 4 ells (1.75) in a continuous row to the end. Thus when something is damaged by the catapult, we can easily repair it." Entirely unlikely is Kangle's adoption of the interpretation of the Malayalam commentary of *tāla-mūla* as adjective to *vapra* in the sense of "shaped like the root of a palm tree, i.e. broad at the base and narrow at the top".

8 rounded merlons (*kapiśīrṣakaiś câcitāgram*; see Fig. 1a).[18] An alternative to a brick wall is a wall of rough stones (*śaila*), which is built of large rocks (*pṛthuśilā-saṃhita*) as known at Rājagṛha
9 (Fig. 2).[19] Owing to the danger of fire, city walls made of timber (*kāṣṭha-maya*) are discouraged. Megasthenes saw such a palisade — the fortification at Pāṭaliputra[20] that, in fact, has also been excavated there[21] (Fig. 3). It was certainly a predecessor of and the model for the brick wall on top of the rampart.[22] The improving

[18] In the manuscripts of the KA., before *kapiśīrṣakaiś* is written *murajakaiḥ* ('with drums') or (manuscripts G and M) *urajakaiḥ* ('with bosoms'). These words seem, like the term *kapiśīrṣaka* itself, to articulate comparisons of the form of the merlons. In the representations of the fortifications at Sanci (see Fig. 1a), this rounded form really comes close to monkey heads, (conic) drums, or bosoms, so that the meaning "merlon" for *kapiśīrṣaka* can be considered certain. The term also occurs in a scene of the play Avimāraka, in which the hero climbs on a rope that he cast over a merlon (p. 46): *aho sthiratvam ucchitatvaṃ prākārasya iha sthitvā rajjuṃ prakṣipāmi (rajjuṃ kṣiptvā) hanta baddhaḥ karkaṭaka-rajjvā kapiśirsakaḥ rajjum avalambyārohāmi.* As a part of the gate, the term *kapiśīrṣaka* has another meaning; it signifies the bolts by means of which the door is made fast. See Coomaraswamy, *Indian Architectural Terms*, JAOS 48, p. 256.

[19] ARASI 1905/06, p. 88: "The faces of the walls are built of massive undressed stones between 3 and 5 feet in length, carefully fitted and bonded together, while the core between them is composed of smaller blocks less carefully cut and laid with chips or fragments of stone packing the interstices between them. No mortar or cement is visible anywhere in the stone work."

[20] According to Megasthenes (in Strabo Fragm. 25,2) these fortifications had embrasures. See Stein, *Megasthenes and Kauṭilya*, p. 29 (transl.): "at the confluence of this (Ganges) and of another river (Erannoboas) lay Palibothra. The length measures 80 stadia, the width 15, in the form of a parallelogram, with a wooden, fenestrated wall so that one could shoot through the holes. In front lay a moat to protect and to accommodate the discharge of the city."

[21] ARASI 1926/27, p. 136f.: "Dr Spooner's excavations had revealed the existence of a long wooden palisade of Mauryan times running W-E from the south of the Bulandi Bagh site for a distance of some 450 feet... It seems to have been a wide wooden wall, hollow inside to serve possibly as a passage. Excavation at its west end has revealed that this wooden wall was originally covered with earth up to a certain height and that probably an opening existed where the sloped or ramped end occurs here. The palisade is constructed of heavy sleepers set at intervals about equal to their width, the sleepers being laid horizontally across the wall to form the top and bottom and vertically to form the two sides.... The width of the palisade across the wooden uprights is about 14´-6", and these uprights were spanned originally at the top by beams, one of which is still in position at the foot of the sloping western end." For this, see Wheeler, in: AI 4, p. 96, "Whether this was a passage within an earth rampart or whether, as more likely, the structure was filled with earth and formed its core or revetment, was not ascertained, although the point is one which could readily be determined by trained observation. "

[22] The name *śāla* (or *sāla*), 'shal-wood (wall)', which can be used synonymously with *prākāra*, shows that the city wall was originally built of wood. See Ch. 1, note 155. In KA. 10,1,1, the army camp, which has to be constructed according to the pattern of a city, should be provided with a moat, a rampart, a *śāla* (wall), gates and towers (*khāta-vapra-sāla-dvārāṭṭalalaka-saṃpanna*). Here, one is not dealing

tactics of siege, such as the use of fire projectiles mentioned in KA. 13,4,15, made the use of wood obsolescent.

The exact data on the size and form of the moats, ramparts, 4-9
and walls permit a graphic rendering of the system of fortifications outlined in the Kauṭilīya (Fig. 4). The cross-section shows that the instructions fully correspond to structural statics and constructional feasibility. The question arises as to what extent they correspond to actual structures. This question is most important in light of the fact that in the Greco-Roman world it was not usual to build a city wall on an artificial rampart, atop an earth wall 10 m high. Likewise, we also find no such ramparts in the Hellenistically inspired building techniques at Taxila.[23] Nor does the natural stone wall in old Rājagṛha stand on an artificial rampart. It continues on the ridge of the mountain that surrounds the city located in the valley as a natural protective wall.[24]

Outside of this valley lies the new Rājagṛha, and here in fact a moat was excavated, as well as a rampart, originally 7.31 m high, upon which was built a brick wall, 3.35 m wide, after a small wall of an earlier period decayed and was demolished (Fig. 5).[25] The

with a brick wall, despite the danger of fire, but rather with a palisade of shalwood, whereas KA. 13,4,9 (*durgaṃ khātasālābhyām*) *sāla* means the brick wall. This holds true also for *anusālaṃ* ('along the wall') KA. 2,4,16 and 12,5,17.

[23] AI 4, p. 44: "Within the width of the main trench the city-wall was a homogeneous structure, without evidence of ancient restoration or of any preceding rampart." p. 46: "The city-wall at this place was 21 feet 4 inches thick; its inner face stood to a height of 9½ feet, and the outer to a height of 2¼ feet.... The wall was a homogeneous structure, being built of rubble with small chips of stone inserted in the interstices." Marshall, *Taxila I*, p. 113: "The stone wall which surrounded the Sirkap city was approximately 6,000 yards or nearly 3½ miles in length, with a thickness varying from 15 to 21 ft. 6 in. " p. 114: "The height of the walls was in all probably between 20 and 30 ft."

[24] AI 7, p. 66: "The valley is surrounded on all sides by hills. ... They provide an excellent natural fortification for the valley they surrounded and this must have been the major factor responsible for its selection as the capital-site of Magadha. At a very early stage in the life of the city the natural defences were substantially re-inforced by a fortification consisting of a high rubble-wall running at the top of all the hills, with a circuit of about 25 miles, and the natural gaps between the hills were utilized as gates in the fortification. Inside the valley were other defensive walls built in different periods, the chief of which was the inner defensive wall, generally built of heaped up earth with a rough rubble-core and enclosing a pentagonal area with a perimeter of 5 miles."

[25] Ind. Arch. 1961/62, p. 7f.: "The basal deposits of the rampart were composed of about 1 m thick yellowish-brown mud with dark bands. Over this deposit was raised the main core of the mud-rampart to a height of 7.31 m and retained on the southern side by a brick wall, standing to a height of 7.31 m and retained on the southern side by a brick wall, standing to a height of 2.13 m, being 1.21 m wide at the top and battered to an angle of 17°. The top of the rampart was hardened by yellowish mud and brickbats. The base of the mud-rampart was available to a width of 40.53 m, but on the northern side it was

planning of the new Rājagṛha seems to be typical of the Indian urban fortifications. In Śrāvastī the earthen rampart, which measured 2.75 m in width, is preserved at different heights up to 19 m.[26] Vaiśālī, a small city,[27] but one famed for its beauty, was enclosed by a moat 38 m wide and a rampart not quite 3 m high, upon which a wall 2.75 m wide was erected later (Fig. 6).[28] The Kaliṅga city Si-

3.04 m less wide. Associated with it was a moat, the full width and depth of which has not been so far determined.... In Period II B a brick fortification-wall was added to the extant top of the mud-rampart. Over the collapsed debris of the brick fortification, a 2.13 m thick deposit of earth mixed with ash was laid in Period III A.... Over the top of this repaired rampart was raised in Sub-Period III B, a 33.5 m (? corr.: 3.35 m) wide wall, built essentially of brick-bats possibly robbed from the remains of the earlier walls and available to a height of 0.38 m."

[26] ARASI 1907/08, p. 84: "Its outline is very distinctly marked by earthen ramparts. These vary considerably in height, those of the west being 35´ to 40´ high, while those on the south and east are not more than 25´ to 40´ high"; p. 88: "The ramparts here rise to a height of 63´"; p. 111: "From the curve of the eastern bastion the city wall was excavated for a distance of 48´, and its top could be traced still further east. Its width is about 9´ and it is built on the top of the earthen ramparts so that its foot is above the level of the surrounding country." IA 1958/59, p. 47: "The excavation revealed that the site had been occupied for a considerably long time, prior to the coming up of the defences"; p. 50: "Period II was marked by the coming up of a mud-rampart, which, with a circuit of 3 miles, was laid roughly in the form of a crescent with the northern side overlooking the river Rapti. Of the rampart and other structures going with it, four Sub-periods were noted. In the earliest Sub-period, the rampart had a basal width of 95 ft. The highest available point where from it sloped either side — the slope of the exterior being steeper was noted to be 12 ft. above the contemporary ground level.... In the second Sub-period was built a brick structure, serving possibly as a parapet over the rampart. In the next Sub-period the height of the rampart was raised by mud-filling, while in the last Sub-period was built a brick structure above that filling."

[27] Krishna Deva and Vijayakanta Mishra, *Vaiśālī Excavations* 1950, *Vaiśālī* 1961, p. 5: "The site of Rājā-Visāla-kā-Garh, hereafter called the garh area, is believed to represent the remains of the citadel or palace of Vaiśālī. It is a large brick-covered mound about a mile in circumference." It is, however, doubtful that Rājā-Visālakā-Garh was only the citadel, while the city itself lay outside the fortifications. The size of the garh area corresponds well with that of a small city, while a palace of this size would be unusual.

[28] *Vaiśālī Excavations*, p. 5: "Originally the whole area was surrounded by a moat having a maximum width of about 125 feet"; p. 3: "The excavations revealed two phases of the defences of the garh site. The first phase is that of a mud-rampart more than 65 feet wide and over 9 feet high, which was followed by a sort of mud-brick structure in the second phase. From the associated finds the construction of the mud-rampart is assignable to Period Ib (c. 300 to 150 B.C.)." IA 1958/59, p. 12: "In Period II the defences consisted of a massive rampart, 68 ft. In width at the base, 21 ft., in width at the extant top and 13 ft. in extant height; it was made of earth, the digging of which left a moat around the fort. A sealing of Agnimitra found in one of the post-rampart layers, with characters of the second century B.C., was a pointer to the date of the erection

supalgarh possessed a mud rampart, exactly quadratic in plan and about 8 m in height, on top of which was erected a mighty wall 10 m wide. At this width, naturally, the wall was not massive, but consisted of two parallel brick walls, with the space in between filled with mud (Fig. 7).[29] In Nagarjunakonda the wall on the rampart was 3-4 m wide; a moat 3.6 m deep and between 20 and 40 m wide surrounded the fortification in the valleys.[30] In the case of Ahicchatra, two chronologically successive earthen ramparts enclosed the city.[31] From Jaugada it is reported that a stone wall stood on the rampart, the height of which measured 4.5 m. The existence of a trench also could be proven here.[32] Bhita possessed on top of

of the rampart. In Period III, probably of the late Kushan and early Gupta age, a brick rampart, 9 ft. wide, was constructed, with military barracks."

[29] AI 5, p. 74f.: "In the earliest phase, the defences consisted of a massive clay-rampart over 25 feet high at his point (as it survived now) and 110 feet wide at the base.... The construction of the rampart was more or less synchronous with the arrival of the black-and-red ware at the site, that is, about 200 B.C.... Phase III witnessed a change in the make-up of the defences. Two brick wall, 26 feet apart and respectively 2 feet 6 inches and 3 feet 6 inches thick (the thicker one being on the outer side), were built at the top of the laterite gravel and the space between them was filled up with mud and earth."

[30] Ind. Arch. 1957/58, p. 5: "Trenches laid across the wall, both on the east and west, showed that it had been built in two phases: the first or lower phase was represented by a rampart of morum or mud, about 80 ft. wide at the base, resting on the natural soil.... The second phase was represented by a burnt-brick wall, 9 to 14 ft. thick, generally built either directly on the existing rampart or on a secondary filling over it, but on naturally high grounds directly on the bare rock-surface. Save for the portion overlying the Peddakundellagutta hill, the fortification-wall was surrounded by a ditch, 12 ft. in depth and varying from 74 to 132 ft. in width."

[31] AI 1, p. 38: "The defences of the city were partially explored at two places and it was revealed that below the brick wall there were two successive earth ramparts. The core of the earlier rampart as well as the soil below it yielded considerable quantities of grey pottery, which, as will be seen below, had been the distinguishing pottery from c. 300 to 100 B.C. Its existence in the core of the rampart suggests that the earlier rampart, the first fortification round the city, was erected not much later than B.C. 100." As opposed to this, M. Wheeler wrote in *Early India and Pakistan*, p. 131f., the following: "Inconclusive excavation in 1940-4 showed two successive earthen ramparts below a stout wall of baked brick and P. G. Ware is said to have been found below, as well as in, the earlier rampart. If so, the rampart should not be later than 400 B.C. and may be somewhat earlier."

[32] Ind. Arch. 1956/57, p. 31: "The following conclusions, based on a preliminary examination of the material so far excavated, are to be regarded as provisional. On the natural soil was a sandy layer with flimsy occupational debris, consisting of sherds of fine black-and-red ware. Over it was built the first defensive rampart, its extant maximum height being 14 ft. 6 in. and basal width 70 ft. The material to form the rampart was obtained by the cutting of a ditch into the sandy layer and the varied natural deposits of clayey earth with kankar nodules, laterite-gravel and stone chips. Thus constituted, the rampart contained stray sherds of the same

the city rampart a wall about 3.4 m thick.[33] The fortification at Charsada was quite small. The trench here was only 4.5 m wide and 3 m deep, and for the earthen rampart, which had entirely disappeared at the places that were excavated, a width of less than 5 m can be assumed.[34] Old Ujjayinī lay with its western flank on the bank of the Sipra. It had a moat 45 m wide and 6.6 m deep on the opposite side; it protected the city on all sides by means of a water barrier behind which rose a city wall over 12 m high (Fig. 8).[35] Remains of a wall on top of this rampart have not yet been reported. In much the same way, Bhārukaccha (Broach) seems to have lacked a wall on top of the rampart; instead the rampart is jacketed with bricks. The most imposing example of such a

nature as the sandy layer. The inner bank of the ditch has been traced in the extreme outer end of the trench, but its width and depth have not been ascertained. The next important phase of the rampart, separated from the initial one by an intermediate phase, during which the existing top was covered by a thick deposit of earth after some occupational layers had accumulated on the inner face, saw the construction of a 2 ft. high wall of rubble and stone chips with a cap of large boulders all laid in thick laterite-gravel and clay — against the inner side."

[33] ARASI 1911/12, p. 29: "The defences were found to consist of a wall, 11´2" thick, raised on an earthen rampart."

[34] Wheeler, *Charsada*, 1962, p. 27: "As it survives, the ditch is not of very impressive size.... it is fair to estimate the original size of the ditch as something like 15 ft. wide and 10 ft. deep.... the ditch was deliberately filled, presumably with its own excavated earth which had doubtless meanwhile done duty as a rampart on the inner margin. This rampart had indeed been completely scraped away on Ch. IIIK.... A series of postholes each a foot in diameter and 1-1 ½ ft. deep, indicated a former timber-lined postern and bridge and suggested that the rampart had in face been some 16 ft. broad. The passage through it had been about 6 ft. wide.... At one point 500 ft. north of our postern it is likely that further excavation may reveal the character of the missing rampart ... The indications were that it had been an earthen mound some 15 ft. wide faced on the outer side with a mudbrick wall 4 ft. thick, the base of which was still in situ." According to Wheeler, the fortification belonged to the second half of the 1st millennium BCE.

[35] Ind. Arch. 1956/57, p. 20: "The rampart, as superficially observed, encloses an area measuring approximately 1 x ¾ mile, with a basal width of a little over 200 ft. and a maximum extant height of 42 ft. ... The rampart was built in Period I by the dumping of dug-up yellow and black clays to form a thick wall with a gentle slope on the inner side and a less-pronounced one on the exterior. As originally planned, it was surrounded on the west and, distantly, on the north by the river Sipra, while a moat, exposed by excavation on the eastern side and found to be filled with greenish water-borne silt, added to it a line of defence in that direction and, presumable, on the south side as well, being apparently connected with the river and thus completing the circuit of a water-barrier. The moat was found to have been at least 80 ft. wide and 22 ft. deep during its functional life." Ind. Arch. 1957/58, p. 34: "The rampart was noted to have been 345 ft. broad at the base, and the surrounding moat 152 ft. wide at the top, in the earliest Period I, datable from circa 700 to 500 B.C." See also the comments of the excavators N.R. Banerjee in his basic work *The Iron Age in India* (New Delhi 1965), p. 15f.

brick-clad rampart[36] came to light in the excavation of Kauśāmbī (Fig. 9).[37] Here the rampart, nearly 13 m high and very steep in the lower fifth, is fortified with 154 layers of bricks. The lower and rather steep brick courses were plastered in order to prevent climbing.[38] An enormous moat with a width of up to 145 m surrounded this old fortress.[39] A smaller version of Kauśāmbī is the city Unchadih, with its brick-clad rampart 9 m high and a moat 7.5 m wide.[40] In Rajghat a rampart about 10 m high is confirmed,[41] as also at Maheshpur[42] and Thanesar.[43] Whether a wall stood on the ram-

[36] Ind. Arch. 1959/60, p. 19: "The first inhabitants of the town appear to have raised a mud-rampart with a deep ditch on the outer side.... The mud-rampart appears to have been provided with heavy brick revetments, which subsequently collapsed in a spread-eagle way. The bricks in these revetments were of the dimensions of either 1 ft. 4 in. X 11 in. x 3 in. , or 1 ft. 1 in. x 8 in. x 2 ½ in."

[37] G.R. Sharma, *The Excavations at Kauśāmbī (1957-59)*. While Sharma, Ind. Arch. 1953/54, p. 9, assumes approximately the 6th century BCE as upper limit for the building of the rampart (Ind. Arch. 1958/59, p. 47: the 1st quarter of the 1st millennium). According to his monograph, the rampart was built and provided with a brick revetment between 1025 and 955 BCE. At the earliest a century later, approximately between 885 and 815 BCE, the moat was excavated.

[38] Ind. Arch. 1957/58, p. 47: "In the earliest period, I, the defences consisted of a mud wall with a burnt-brick revetment on the exterior, the latter being available to a height of 42 ft. 5 in. and comprising one hundred and fifty-four courses of bricks. The first thirty courses from the bottom showed a batter of about 15° from the vertical and the upper courses 40°, the bricks being laid through in the English bond. Up to the first thirty courses the revetment was also covered by a 2 to 2 ½ in thick mud plaster." In subsequent periods the wall was repaired and enlarged several times. See Sharma, *The Excavations at Kauśāmbī*, p. 27ff.

[39] Sharma, *The Excavations at Kauśāmbī*, p. 38: "The total width of the moat in this area is 480 ft." IA 1954/55, p. 18: "a 300 ft. wide moat".

[40] Ind. Arch. 1959/60, p. 46: "Unchadih had clear traces of a fortified habitation, 170 x 110 ft., with corner-towers — a small scale replica of Kauśāmbī. The rampart was 30 ft. in height and was brick-faced on the outer side. There were signs of a moat, about 25 ft. wide, with watch-towers on its outer side."

[41] Ind. Arch. 1960/61, p. 37: "It was revealed that the earliest occupation of the site went back to the first quarter of the first millennium B.C.... The most noteworthy discovers of the season was that of an enormous clay rampart dating back to the earliest occupation of the site. Built directly over the natural soil and available to a height of about 10 meters, the rampart has a pronounced slope towards the river. Other details of the rampart, including its correlation with the habitational levels, however, remain to be determined." IA 1961/62, p. 58: "It was observed that the rampart had two structural phases. In the earlier phase, it was made of rammed compact brownish clay, with a basal width of 19.80 m and rising to an extant height of 5.10 m, with a pronounced outer slope. In the succeeding phase, it was heightened by a 1.10 m thick mud-filling."

[42] ARASI 1924/25, p. 90: "Between the Karatoya and the Teesta lies a big rampart ..." On examination it was found to be a high mud wall a hundred feet in thickness, generally twenty to forty feet in height above the cultivated fields at the back and forty to sixty feet from the bed of the fosse or moat in front of it."

[43] ASIR, Vol. II, 1871, p. 220: "It is said to have had 52 towers or bastions, of which some remains still exist. On the west side the earthen ramparts rise to a

part here remains an open question. The same can be said for Mathurā, where the site report speaks of two rings of clay ramparts of which the outer one reportedly encloses the city itself and the inner one the citadel inside.[44]

When we compare the excavation results with the instructions of the Kauṭilīya, we see that not only the conception of a defensive system of moat, rampart and wall, but also the dimensions given in the Kauṭilīya generally correspond to those of archaeo-
4 logical discoveries. It is striking that the Kauṭilīya prescribes a triple system of moats with a total width of 68.40 m and a depth of 18.90 m.[45] Kauśāmbī had multiple moats with a total width of 145 m, and, according to Megasthenes, Pāṭaliputra possessed a moat 177.60 m wide.[46] The depth mentioned in the Kauṭilīya, however, is remarkable. The reason for this prescription is probably to protect the fortress from undermining. Whether this depth was realized in any fortification requires further study. At any rate, the amount of earth produced through the excavation of the moat would produce much more earth than necessary for the building of the rampart. The Kauṭilīya, consequently, adds that

height of 60 feet above the road, but the mass of the interior is not more than 40 feet high."

[44] Ind. Arch. 1954/55, p. 15: "Furthermore, an exploratory survey revealed the existence of two rings of mud-ramparts, the first elliptical in shape and the second quadrangular and comprised within the first, as if signifying a citadel." See also Stuart Piggott, *Some Ancient Cities of India*, Oxford 1945, p. 45: "I think it probable that it is to the Kushan period that we should attribute the great city walls that enclose an elongated horseshoe-shaped area based on the right bank of the Jumna.... Today the walls are a string of irregular mounds of clay and earth, but it is possible to see in sections cut through them that they originally consisted of a mud-brick wall probably twenty feet thick and fifty or more feet high backed by a substantial earthen rampart. The square Katra area is enclosed with similar walls, with indications of towers at the angles, and may have constituted a citadel within the main city walls."

[45] Also Philon of Byzantium prescribes a triple moat in front of the city wall. In this case, however, the moats should be much further apart, and the space between them should be filled with the piled up earth, palisades, and thorn hedges. See H. Diels and E. Schramm, *Exzerpte aus Philons Mechanik B VII and VIII*, p. 34 (69) (translated): "For all fortifications not fewer than three moats are to be excavated. The first should be at a distance of one plethron (100´= 29.57 m) from the wall, the second at a distance of 40 ells (17.74 m) from that one, and the third at the same distance from the second" (72): "One must make the moats as deep as possible and the breadth not less than 70 ells (31 m)." The purpose of this spread system of moats was especially for protection from ballistic machines. The city Sirynx serves as an example of such a system (see Polybios X, 31, transl. H. Drexler, in *Bibliographie der Alten Welt*, Vol. I, p. 722: "The city had three moats, each not less than 30 ells wide and 15 ells deep. On their banks rose double palisades and behind them a strong wall."

[46] Cf. O. Stein, p. 38; see Ch. 1, p. 27.

the remaining earth (*pāṃśu-śeṣeṇa*)[47] irregularities in the building area (*vāstu-cchidra*) should be filled. 5

The description of the Kauṭilīya next turns to defenses that 10-15
are linked to the walls. First, a tower (*aṭṭālaka*)[48] should be 10
erected every 54 m. It should have a rectangular foundation (*viṣkambha-caturaśra*) and trap-stairs parallel with its vertical axis (*utsedhasamāvakṣepa-sopāna*).[49] The rectangular plan of the towers is evident at Kauśāmbī,[50] Bhita (Fig. 10),[51] old Rājagṛha (Fig. 11),[52] Taxila/Sirkap (Fig. 12),[53] and the palace fortress at

[47] The reading *pāṃśu-viśeṣeṇa* (G M) is secondary. Meyer's and Stein's translations, which are based on this reading, are incorrect. Meyer (translated): "he should fill the holes of the construction site with any sort of soil". Stein (translated): "or he should fill the holes of the construction site with especially fine dust" and in the associated footnote: "The purpose being, it seems, that an enemy who advances there will sink in." Kangle provides the correction: "*vastucchidram* refers to areas in the city unsuitable for building purposes because they are not level".

[48] The term *aṭṭala(ka)* occurs frequently in city descriptions, by which is intended sometimes towers linked to gate structures (*dvārāṭṭālaka, gopurāṭṭālaka*) and sometimes towers located between the gates (*antarāṭṭālaka*). The kinds of towers are not described in detail. Only in one place in a Jātaka verse (Jāt. VI,269,7) towers are compared to the necks of camels (*aṭṭālakā oṭṭhagīviyo*). Thus, the poet seems to refer to round towers.

[49] While *sama-caturaśra* designates a quadrangle with equal (*sama*) sides, i.e., a square, *viṣkambha-caturaśra* seems to designate a quadrangle in which the length (*viṣkambha*) of two sides is determined separately from the other two, i.e., a rectangle (=*dīrgha-caturaśra*). Not so Kangle: "*viṣkambhacaturaśram* a square with the width (of the parapets); the turret is thus a square structure, each side being as long as the parapet-width". Archaeological contexts show, however, that the side lengths of towers are always wider than the width of the walls.

[50] Ind. Arch. 1956/57, p. 28: "Excavation of a 65 ft. high tower in the eastern rampart revealed that initially the bastion, like the rampart itself, had been of mud. At the top of the bastion was erected a central tower, 38 x 11 ft., flanked by projecting platforms on the eastern and western sides and by guard-rooms on the other sides."

[51] ARASI 1911/12, p. 29: "a quadrangular bastion,... which projects 15´ from the outer curtain of the wall and measures 31 feet along its face.... The bastion is standing to a height of 6´ to 9´ above its base, which was 13´ below the surface of the mound."

[52] ARASI 1905/06, p. 88: "A noticeable feature of the fortifications is bastions attached to the outside of the walls wherever especial strength was required. Sixteen such structures have been observed... They are solid rectangular buildings, constructed after the same fashion as the wall and built on to it at irregular intervals. In plan, they measure from 47´ to 60´ long by 34´ to 40´ broad, the long side always coinciding with the face of the wall on to which they abut. They rise to the same height as the wall, and like it, were, no doubt, provided with superstructures which have now disappeared. The distances between the bastions on the west of the Bagaṅgā defile are 80´, 168´ and 185´ respectively, those on the east being 140´ and 146´."

[53] AI 4, p. 42 (Sirkap): "Projecting bastions occur at frequent but irregular intervals. Most of them are square on plan, but at the angles of the wall they

Pāṭaliputra.[54] A tower represented in a relief at Sanci, moreover, is rectangular in shape (Fig. 13), whereas towers in Gandharan art are sometimes rendered round (Fig. 14) and sometimes squarish (Fig. 28). The observation regarding the trap-stairs can perhaps be understood to mean that the towers, as at Dura Europos,[55] were only accessible by means of ladders. If the enemy could conquer a part of the wall, then the ladders should be retracted and the success of the conquerors impeded.[56] The distance between towers follows the classical rule[57] that it should not to be greater than an arrow-shot.[58] This rule corresponds well to the prescription of a distance of 54 m in the Kauṭilīya.

assume an unusual pentagonal shape, completely revealed at the north-east corner in 1945." On the other hand, at Sirukh the bastions were semicircular. See Marshall, *Taxila I*, p. 218: "Along the outer curtain of the wall and separated from each other by intervals of about 90 ft. are semi-circular bastions, access to the interior of which is provided by a narrow passage carried through the thickness of the wall."

[54] ARASI 1914/15, p. 16: "At site no. V last year I had found a short stretch of a massive wall which appeared to be part of the main rampart which I was endeavouring to prove as a boundary to the palace precincts as such.... The wall now has been cleared on both sides and has been found to be a true rampart, having originally supported rectangular turrets like those depicted in the most ancient Indian sculptures of palace walls."

[55] The Excavations at Dura-Europos, 4th Season 1930/31, p. 6: "In times of peace, the garrison could only reach the city by ladders placed at these points; in case of sedition, it was easy to remove them, thus isolating the fortifications."

[56] Vitruvius I,V,4 for the same reason prescribes building of retractable beam passages (ed. Fensterbusch p. 56): *Etiamque contra inferiores [partes] turrium dividends est murus intervallis tam magnis, quam erunt turres, ut itinera sint interiorbus partibus turrium contignata, neque ea ferro fixa; hostis enim si quam partem muri occupaverit, qui repugnabunt rescindent et, si celeriter adminstraverint, non partientur reliquas partes turrium murique hostem penetrare, nisi se voluerit praecipitare*; (translated): "Towards the lower parts of the towers, the wall must have cavities as wide as the towers so that gangways made of beams can be installed inside the towers. These gangways should not be anchored by iron cramps. Thus, if the enemy were to occupy any part of the wall, the defenders can destroy (the gangways), and if this is quickly done, it obstructs the enemy from entering the other parts of the towers and walls, if they don't want to plunge deep head first."

[57] Vitruvius I,V,4, ed. C. Fensterbusch p. 56: *Intervalla autem turrium ita sunt facienda, ut ne longius sit alia ab alia sagittae missionis, uti, si qua oppugnetur, tum a turribus, quae erunt destra sinistra, scorpionibus reliquisque telorum missionibus hostes reiciantur*; (translated): "The spaces between the towers are to be constructed in a way that one tower is not farther than a bowshot away from the other. Thus, if a tower is attacked, the enemy can be driven back by the use of scorpions and other catapults from the towers left and right of that one."

[58] H. Droysen, *Heerwesen and Kriegführung der Griechen*, p. 22 note 1 gives (according to Strabo) "at least 50 m" as the range of an arrow-shot. Distances that exceed this distance (up to 180 m) are to be regarded only as the maximal accomplishment of excellent archers.

Based on the information provided by Megasthenes with regard to the circumference and the number of defensive towers and gates of Pāṭaliputra, a distance of 53 m between the towers and between towers and gates can be calculated.[59] In Bhita the distance between the excavated tower and the city gate amounts to about 55 m. In Rājagṛha and Taxila, the position of the towers is dictated by the topography, and the distance from each other thus is not uniform.

After discussing the towers, the Kauṭilīya addresses the pos- 11
tern gates (*pratolī*),[60] which are located between two towers and
which, including a two-storied upper floor (*saharmya-dvitala*), are
to be 1½ times as long as wide. This does not seem to describe
the city gates per se, since these are subjected later on to an extensive description. [61] One must think of pedestrian gateways that
were equipped for their defense with a superstructure (*harmya*).
Such a structure is represented on a relief in Sanci (Fig. 15).
Archaeological evidence is lacking for the time being.[62] In the 12
interstices between the towers and postern gates (*aṭṭālaka-pratoli-
madhye*) embrasures (*indrakośa*)[63] are to be inserted, which
are covered with wooden shutters with loopholes (*sāpidhāna-
cchidra-phalaka-sahita*).[64] These serve as the location for three
archers (*tridhanuṣkādhisthāna*). The "path of the [war]god" 13

[59] Cf. Stein, p. 31. The length was 80 stadia = 14208 m and the width 15 stadia = 2664 m. Thus the circumference was 33744 m. The wall had 570 towers and 64 gates, which amounts to a distance between towers and gates of 53 m. Stein, however (p. 36), arrives at a different conclusion, because he neglects to add the distance between towers and gates to the distance between the towers.

[60] In the Kośas *pratolī* is mistakenly designated as "street" (*pratolī rathyā Nīlakaṇṭha: abhyantara-mārga. Śabdakalpadrūma; rathyā-pratolī-viśikhāḥ samāḥ,* etc.). J.Ph. Vogel JRAS 1906, p. 539ff. (see Album Kern, p. 235ff.) showed that *pratolī* is a kind of gate. It has also survived in recent Indian languages with this same meaning.

[61] This city gate itself also bears a name that is combined with *pratolī*. But its meaning is obscure: *pratolī-ṣaṭṭulantaram dvāraṃ*, "a tower with the space of six beams of a tower-gate".

[62] However, narrow postern gates through a wall that are only negotiable by pedestrians are evident in several fortresses. See IA 1957/58, p. 5 (Sisupalgarh): "a narrow postern gate, on the northern side, possibly serving as an emergency-exit". AI 5, p. 64 (Sisupalgarh): "eight large gateways, two on each side, besides about the same number of smaller openings distributed all over the perimeter". Sharma, *The Excavations at Kauśāmbī*, p. 24: "There were six subsidiary gateways — two in each wing."

[63] Kangle: "a board, compact with planks having holes with coverings". Meyer (translated): "a veranda with roofing and perforated beams".

[64] Boards that served as shutters and at the same time offered protection against enemy missiles are represented in the depiction of the doors in the Sanci reliefs (see Fig. 16). In the Gandhara image of a fortification wall as well (Fig. 14), they seem to be located along the wall.

14 (*deva-patha*) is best explained as the path along the wall behind the embrasures.[65] Ways (*caryā*)[66] are to be laid 1.8 m to 3.6 m apart from each other (*daṇḍāntarā dvidaṇḍāntarā vā*), as well as runways (*pradhāvanikā*)[67] and sortie-doors (*niṣkira-dvāra*)[68] at an
15 impregnable place (*agrāhye deśe*).[69] Outside (*bahir*) runs a concealed path (*channa-patha*), which is protected by barbed wire, pits, and the like. Perhaps this path is identical with a walled subterranean passage that came to light in Kauśāmbī in front of the rampart.[70]

16-22 The remainder of the chapter contains a detailed treatment of the city gates. The gate structures were of such importance that they required the full attention of the architect of the fortifications. If the enemy were to penetrate the gates, the entire effort in constructing the enormous rampart and wall would become useless. In times of peace gates had to be ready for use by carriages and elephants, but during a time of war they had to be an impregnable barrier for attackers. Several relief representations of Indian gates have survived. The type of gate represented in Sanci (Fig. 16) occurs again with hardly any change at Amaravati (Fig. 17).

[65] The term *devapatha*, which also occurs in Pāṇini V,3,100, corresponds to *indrapatha* in Avim. (p. 47: a*ṭṭāla-pratolīndrapathebhyaḥ*). Unfortunately, the statement of its dimensions is extremely puzzling: "in the gaps 90 cm wide and on the side four times the length" (*antareṣu dvihasta-viskambhaṃ pārśve caturguṇāyāmaṃ*).

[66] Kangle: " '*caryāḥ* tracks, courses' seems to refer to steps for going up and down from the *devapatha* to the *pradhāvanikā*. The tracks would naturally be well protected as they are apparently on the outside of the wall."

[67] Kangle: "G M *pradhāvitikāṃ*". Kangle translates: "a run-way". Meyer (translated): "a way to the attack". Konow, *Kauṭalya Studies*, p. 63: "place of refuge".

[68] Kangle: "G *niṣkura-* M *niṣkuru* (M_2 *°ṣkara*), Cb *niṣkuha*". Kangle translates: "an exit door"; Meyer (translated): " a sally port". The meanings of this and the preceding term are uncertain. The term *niṣkira* appears again KA. 13,4,12 in the rules for the siege of a fort: *niṣkirād upaniṣkṛṣyāśvaiś ca prahareyuḥ*. Kangle: "Dragging out (soldiers) from the run-way exit, they should strike with horses."

[69] However, ed. Shamasastri and Jolly: *āgrāhye deśe*, "on a pregnable (=vulnerable) place". Kangle does not cite this reading.

[70] Sharma, *The Excavations at Kauśāmbī*, pl. 32f.: "Over the debris of Wall 4 was built Wall 6, measuring 63 ft. 3 ins. and 67 ft. 10 ins. respectively, on the inner and outer (city) sides of the curve. It was 6 ft. 10 ins. wide and encased a stone-paved passage, 6 ft. 10 ins. deep and 1 ft. 9 ins. wide.... The passage (or drain?) had a corbelled arch finally capped with bricks laid width-wise. At either end of this passage was a pair of slits, 2.5 ins. wide and 3.5 ins. set inside the walls, into which planks may have been inserted. In the curved wall, two man-holes (possibly ventilators) (2 ft. x 2 ft.) divide the extant length into three nearly equal parts. It appears to have been a passage and not a drain because the level of the pavement is higher in the middle and has a gradual slope of only 1 in. towards the two ends. There is no opening in the wall in the middle and it could not have received any drain-water from any area. The subsequent filling in the passage, was also not the usual stuff of drains. The passage may have served as a secret underground tunnel."

It consists of a multi-storied broad-house with a vaulted roof and two gabled towers quadratic in plan that flank the entrance. The floor plan (Fig. 18) reveals the military weakness of such a structure: the gate-room of the broad-house is too small to stop a determined attacker. If battering rams or elephants had already penetrated, a flood of attackers would pour into the city.[71] Only a long gate-room that could be closed off outside and inside like a sluice offered effective protection. If the attacker forced the outer gate, he would then be captured in the gate chamber, as if in a mousetrap. Such long gate-rooms were found in all Indian city-gates hitherto excavated; in Sisupalgarh (Fig. 19),[72] as well as in Śrāvastī (Fig. 20),[73] Nagarjunakonda (Fig. 21),[74] Taxila (Fig. 22),[75]

[71] Literature records several instances of elephants used to demolish city gates, e.g., Mahāvaṃsa XXV,38 (p. 201); Jāt. II, p. 94f.; Buddhacarita V,82.

[72] AI 5, p. 75ff.: "As stated elsewhere, the fort had eight large gateways, two on each site. Of these, the one nearer the north-west corner on the western side was taken up for excavation. Here the two ends of the main defensive wall turned outwards and each joined the heel of a massive L-shaped gateway-flank built of laterite blocks of an average size of 6 x 2 x 1 feet. The longer arm of the flank measured 160 feet and the shorter one 63 feet, while the width was roughly uniform, being 27-28 feet. The passage flanked by the two longer arms took the form of a slow-rising ramp, about 25 feet wide. Though it provided a straight access to the interior of the fort, the entire system was well-organized from the defensive point of view."

[73] ARASI 1907/08, p. 111ff. (Nausahra Gate): "My excavations have proved that this was one of the main gates of the city. On both sides the city walls curve inwards, so as to form two bastions leaving a space of 60´ in width between. ... It will be noticed that in the above description no mention has been made of an actual structural gateway. There is, however, adjoining the western bastion, a piece of masonry, 6´ wide, which seems to have belonged to such a building. There is nothing corresponding on the east side and the remains in question are too shapeless to allow us to speak with certainty. At any rate it is surely on this spot that the city gate must once have stood. Immediately to the south of the supposed gateway we notice the foundation walls of two distinct rectangular rooms enclosed by solid walls and leaving a passage of about 20´ between. ... the width of each room is from 8´ to 9´... From their position we may infer that these chambers served to accommodate the guard in charge of the gate, but no objects were found to confirm this conjecture."

[74] Ind. Arch. 1957/58, p. 5f. "Two main gateways, one each on the eastern and western sides, and a narrow postern gate, on the northern side, possibly serving as an emergency-exit, were exposed. Close to the eastern gateway were barracks including stables and a nicely plastered masonry cistern. The western gateway, which a minimum width of 17 ft., lay near the *aśvamedha*-site excavated last year."

[75] Marshall, *Taxila I*, p. 115: "The plan of the gatehouse is problematical, as nothing more than its foundations have survived, and these not in their entirety. It appears, however, to have comprised: (a) A large hall, constituting the gateway proper, with an inside measurement of about 62 ft. north and south by 35 ft. east and west. This hall projected about 20 ft. on both sides of the wall.... (b) Two guardrooms set against the outer face of the wall and communicating with the barbican on its western side. (c) Two more guardrooms, with sleeping-cells are positioned against the inner face of the wall, to the west of the gateway."

Thanesar,[76] Paharpur,[77] and probably also in Bhita (Fig. 23).[78] In terms of its plan, this gate form corresponds to those of the Hellenistic world (Fig. 24 and 25). Characteristic of all these gates is a frontal entrance that, as opposed to a lateral entrance, has the advantage that it allows traffic without hindrance. On the other hand, the lateral entrance (Fig. 26) provided a military advantage because it made the attackers expose their unguarded flank to the defenders. In ancient India only a single lateral entrance has been excavated (Fig. 27).[79] Beside the gate depictions in Sanci and Amaravati, the Gandhara reliefs also show a frontal entrance in which the city gate is stylized as a house or cloister door (Fig. 28). In the representation from Mathura of a city, one recognizes a frontal entrance that is flanked by two towers (Fig. 29).

Only by keeping in mind the necessities of fortification and the archaeological finds of gates is it possible to penetrate the
16 description of the Kauṭilīya. This gate description begins with the basic information as to position, size, and form of the plan. After one has built the wall (*prākāram*) on both sides (*ubhayato*) 2.7 m (*adhyardha-daṇḍam*) round (*maṇḍalakam*), one should insert (*niveṣayet*) a gate structure (*pratolī-ṣaṭṭulāntaram dvāram*) into

[76] ARASI 1922/23, p. 90: "I have however definitely located one of the original gates on the west side of the fort. It consists of a broad passage flanked by solidly built brick bastions which presumably gave access to one of the main streets of the fort, as remains of buildings are clearly seen for a considerable distance along it."

[77] ARASI 1925/26, p. 111: "The main entrance was a large hall measuring 49 ft. 6 inches by 47 feet with its roof supported on four rows each consisting of four stone pillars or pilasters. The hall was open towards the north but enclosed on the other sides by heavy walls, access being obtained to the interior of the quadrangle through a single doorway measuring 12 ft. 11 inches in the back or south wall."

[78] Cf. ARASI 1911/12, p. 29ff. The ground plan shows only few structural remains, which are too uncertain to identify as the form of the gate.

[79] This is the eastern gate at Kauśāmbī, which Sharma described in Ind. Arch. 1954/55, p. 18 in the following fashion: "A distinctive feature of the eastern gate was the presence of a curtain in the form of a mud-bund, 305 ft. in length and 72 ft. in average width; between it and the rampart was a passage 25 ft. wide. Beyond the curtain and separated from it by a 300 ft. wide moat were two small mounds serving as watch-towers. Though only a portion of the northern side of the gateway was laid bare this year, this, together with the observation of certain brick-robbings, was sufficient to allow a few inferences about the plan of the gateway. The northern wall, 262 ft. in length and in width ranging from 5 ft. 4 in. to 6 ft. 6 in. in different sub-periods, its southern face remaining in the same plumb throughout, and the extensively-robbed western wall, traced to a length of 44 ft., beyond which it had been washed away by a deep rain gully, met each other at right angles. A third wall, the existence of which was revealed in recent brick-robbings, was noticed to start with the other end of the curtain and run across the rampart. It appeared likely, therefore, that these three walls represented the three sides of the gate, the curtain completing the system at the exterior."

the defensive wall.[80] This gate should form a quadrangle in plan 9 m and 14.4 m wide (*pañcadaṇḍād ekottaram āṣṭa-daṇḍād iti caturaśram*). It should be ⅙ (*ṣaḍ-bhāgam*) or ⅛ (*aṣṭa-bhāgaṃ vā*) longer than wide (*āyāmād adhikam*). Again, the statement of the measurements are exact to such a degree that it enables a graphic reconstruction of the ground plan (Fig. 30).[81] The observation that we are dealing with a quadrangle (*caturaśra*) leaves no doubt that here the Kauṭilīya is not referring to a gate with a broadhouse and two-gabled towers as depicted in the reliefs but rather to the rectangular house-form.[82] A further interesting detail is the information with regard to the curvature of the rampart next to the gate. Evidently, the copyists and commentators no longer recognized the meaning of *maṇḍalakam* and corrected it to *maṇḍakam, maṇḍapakam, meṇḍakam* or *meṇḍhakam,*[83] while architecture manuals preserved the form *maṇḍalakam.*[84] The meaning of this term is clear, if one compares the gate at Śrāvastī, (Fig. 20).[85] Here the gate building does not protrude outward. The wall on both sides curves inward so that the gate house

[80] See Ch. 2, note 61.

[81] The next sentence, which fixes that the determines the shooting level (*talotsedha*) at 15 to 18 *hasta,* clearly shows that the dimensions can only describe the plan of the entire gate-structure, and not, as Meyer believes, that it designates the width and height of the door wings. Stein's remarks in *Arthaśāstra and Śilpaśāstra,* p. 485 rest on the same misunderstanding.

[82] In his study *Early Indian Architecture I. Cities and City-Gates* (EA II, 1930, p. 213ff.), A.K. Coomaraswamy dealt with the gates in the Sanci reliefs. In this study he imposes some terms of our chapter on the ground-plan of this gate, completely ignoring the information of the text concerning the dimensions, as well as the textual and grammatical connections. The information of the KA. with regard to the quadratic form of the plan, besides several other details, shows the impossibility of a procedure of this kind.

[83] Kangle: "G_1 *maṇḍalakam,* G_2M *maṇḍakam,* Cb *maṇḍapakam,* Cj *meṇḍakam*". On the strength of the commentaries, Kangle gives in his text the form *meṇḍhaka.* In his translation Kangle explains in a footnote: "*meṇḍhakam:* there is little doubt about this being the original reading. According to Cnn Cj, it refers to a structure on the rampart on both sides of the gate-way, resembling a ram's head with two horns." However, the context shows that the text deals not with a structure connected with the wall, but rather with the wall itself. How one is to understand this as a ram-head remains just as inexplicable as the purpose that such a construction would serve. Purely decorative elements lie outside of the scope of the Arthaśāstra. Meyer retains the reading *maṇḍalakam* and understands this as a round hole in the wall (? *prākāram*!). So also Shamasastri. Sorabji notes, "making the rampart bulge out to the extent of half a *daṇḍa* on both sides (i.e. outside and inside)".

[84] Mayamata 23,8 (p. 148) = Śilparatnākara 40,7 (p. 203): *antar maṇḍalakam kuryāt;* cf. 40, 27: *kṛtvântaramaṇḍale;* 40,35: *antarmaṇḍal-bhittes.*

[85] See Ch. 2, note 73. When the excavation report says, "On both sides the city-walls curve inward" these words could as well be a translation of *prākāram ubhayato maṇḍalakaṃ kṛtvā.*

is located behind it. This concave wall, which is mentioned in the Kauṭilīya and realized in Śrāvastī, gives the defenders an important strategic advantage in that they can rake the attackers with fire from both sides.

17 After describing the foundation, the Kauṭilīya turns to the
ground floor of the gatehouse with a height between 7.65 m
and 8.1 m (*pañcadaśa-hastād ekottaram aṣṭadaśa-hastād iti*). The
18 circumference (*parikṣepa*) of the bearing columns (*stambha*)
should be 1/6 of their length (*ṣaḍ-āyāma*);[86] their anchoring in the
ground (*nikhāta*) is double (*dviguṇa*), and their capitals (*cūlikā*)
one quarter (*catur-bhāga*). With regard to the gatehouses, only
in Parharpur are columns mentioned,[87] while the upper stories
of the remaining gates rest on the carrying wall. The five parts
19 (*pañca bhāgāḥ*) of the ground floor (*ādi-talasya*) consist of a gate
room (*śālā*), well (*vāpī*), border room (*sīmā-gṛha*) and two plat-
20 forms opposite each other (*dvau pratimañcau*), which comprise
1/10 of the room (*daśa-bhāgikau*). Possibly these platforms served as loading docks for the customs controls. The border room — a secondary room for customs officials and watchmen — is documented in Sisupalgarh (Fig. 19),[88] Thanesar,[89] and Taxila[90] in the right flank of the gate viewed from the outside. By means of its position on the right side, this room at the same time has a military significance. From here the gate garrison could hit the entering enemy on their right side, which was not protected by the shield. The well mentioned in the text came to light in

[86] Vitruvius III,3,10, ed. Fensterbusch p. 149f. gives the circumference for different kinds of Greek columns, which is between 1/8 and 1/10 of their length. Hence such columns were somewhat slimmer.

[87] See Ch 2. note 77.

[88] AI 5, p. 77: "Immediately behind the first gate, and built into the southern flank, was a room (?), 9 ¾ feet long and 6 feet wide." N.: "The western end of the southern flank had largely been destroyed and no more than the foundation-slabs were available. Hence it was difficult to ascertain whether it was really a room or an ancillary passage similar to the one adjacent to the inner gate. However, this point can be verified if another gate is excavated." Viewed from the entrance the southern flank here is the right flank.

[89] ARASI 1922/23, p. 90: "The right-hand bastion, which was partly excavated, appears to consist of small chamber with a narrow entrance."

[90] Marshall, *Taxila I*, p. 115: "(b) Two guardrooms set against the outer face of the wall and communicating with the barbican on its western side. (c) Two more guardrooms, with sleeping-cells against the inner face of the wall, to the west of the gateway. From the excessive strength of their construction it may be inferred that these possessed at least one upper story which communicated directly with the battlements." Again, viewed from the entrance, the western flank is the right flank.

Paharpur[91] and Taxila.[92] For now, position of the subsequently
mentioned interior lateral room (?) (*antaram āṇi-harmyaṃ*)[93] re- 21
mains unclear, as does the pillar construction (*sthūṇā-bandha*) 22
that is half the surface (*ardha-tale*) from the perspective of its
elevation (*samucchrayād*).[94]

The text then proceeds to the upper story (*uttamāgāra*). It should comprise half of the constructed surface (*ardha-vāstuka*) or one-third of the surface area (*tribhāgāntaraṃ vā*), and its side walls should be made of bricks (*iṣṭakāvabaddha-pārśvaṃ*). On the left (*vāmataḥ*) a staircase with a right-hand turn (*pradakṣina-sopāna*) leads down from this upper story and on the other side (*itarataḥ*) a staircase with a light wall covering it (*gūḍhabhitti-sopāna*).[95] If we turn to the plan of the gates at Sisupalgarh (Fig. 19), we find this information confirmed in a startling way. Viewed from the entrance, the right staircase that leads to the upper story is concealed by a wall.[96]

Then follows an enumeration of the individual parts of the 23-28
area in front of the gatehouse: the gate arch head 90 cm wide
(*dvihastam toraṇa-śirah*)[97], the two door wings ⅗ wide[98] (*tripañca-*

[91] ARASI 1925/26, p. 112: "Behind the narrow entrance in the back wall of the gateway we came upon a small chamber from which two or three steps led down to a small tank or reservoir. This small chamber is also open on one side, its roof being supported on two pillars and two pilasters."

[92] Marshall, *Taxila I*, p. 116: "In the main entrance are the remains of two small wells constructed of rubble stone."

[93] The reading is uncertain. Cf. Kangle: "D *antaram āṇi*, G M *antarām āṇi* [em.]."

[94] Cf. Kangle, note: "according to Cnn this describes the *dvitīyatala*, i.e., the first floor.

[95] The term *gūḍhabhiti-sopāna* in the sense of "having a staircase hidden behind the wall" occurs in the KA. 1,20,2 in a description of the *mohana-gṛha*. See G. Roth, *Mohanagṛha, Festschrift Weller*, p. 539 (translated): "with hidden wall stairs".

[96] The medieval Indian architecture manuals frequently repeat the statement that one staircase should be hidden and another in plain view. Cf. Śilparatnākara 22, 205 (p. 136): *agrasopāna-karaṇaṃ guhyāyuhyam iti dvidhā*, Śilparatnākara 5,18; Mayamata 10, 40: *gopura-maṇḍapa-yuktam sopānaṃ acchannam acchannam*; Mayamata 10,94: *ayugmam eva sopānam guhyāguhya-vaśāt tataḥ*; Mayamata 29,54-72: *guhyam sopānam … prādakṣinyena sopānam.*

[97] The opening of the gate was vaulted and served as the upper lintel of the doors.

[98] Contra Meyer (translated): "Three fifths (of the width of the gatehouse)"; Kangle, note: "For their movement when opening or closing, three fifth of the area would seem to be quite necessary." That the ⅗ deals with the frontage of the gatehouse is confirmed by the plan of the northwest gate at Sisupalgarh. Here the entrance comprises ⅗ (4 m) of the inner room between the projecting towers (7 m) (Fig. 19). The representations of the gateways on the Sanci reliefs presuppose the same proportions (Fig. 18).

bhāgikau dvau kapāṭa-yogau), two cross-bars[99] (*dvau*[100] *parighau*), a threshold an ell long (*aratnir indrakīlaḥ*),[101] a side door 2.25 m high (*pañcahastam āṇidvāram*),[102] and four elephant bars (*catvāro hasti-parighāḥ*)[103] across the door leaves [panels?] on the outside of the gate-house, serving as reinforcement against the assault of
29-30 elephants. The causeway (*saṃkrama*)[104] over the moat to the gate, whose width corresponds to the gate opening (*mukha-sama*),

[99] In Rām. 5,53,39 Hanuman invaded Laṅka, grasps the iron-clad (*kālāyasa-pariṣkṛtam*) bar of the gate and kills the guard with it. Hence, one assumes that these blocking beams were not integral part of the door, but rather were detachable. The representation of a town of hungry ghosts on a wall-painting in East Turkistan (A. Grünwedel, *Alt-Kutscha*, Berlin 1920, pl. 16; see Schlingloff, *Religion des Buddhismus II*, Berlin 1963, Fig. 1) shows a cross bar of this kind that does not secure the door from the inside, but rather from the outside in order to lock the hungry ghosts inside the township.

[100] Kangle: "G M *dvau dvau*." This reading, which requires two blocking beams for each door, also rests on the paraphrase of this place in the architecture manual Mayamata 10,41 (p. 43): *dvikavāṭa-catuṣparighārgala-hastonnatendrakīla-yutam*.

[101] Cf. Meyer (translated): "Indra-wedge (*indrakīla*) is the wedge that is placed beneath the two mighty doors where they meet, so that they are more stout." Indrakīla (Pāli *indakhīla*) occurs especially in Buddhist texts (see CPD, BHSD) where it generally means the threshold.

[102] Meyer, note (translated): "This side door is necessary so that one need not always open the unwieldy main gate." The term *āṇi-dvāra* is found also in the chapter on building rules for private houses. KA. 3,8,15: *kiṣku-mātram āṇi-dvāram antarikāyāṃ khaṇḍa-phullārtham asaṃpātaṃ kārayet*, Kangle: "He should cause to be made a side-door in the intervening lane, measuring one *kiṣku*, for making repairs to what is damaged, not (allowing) crowding." In Pāli, *āṇi-dvāra* occurs in Theragāthā 355b where the commentary explains it to be a 'small door of a walled city' *pākāra-baddhassa nagarassa khuddaka-dvāraṃ*, Th-a 151, 8.

[103] Kangle: "The purpose of these, as Cj says, is to prevent the gate being broken down by elephants. They seem to be iron stakes fixed in the gates on the outside." Doors fitted with iron spikes are known from medieval times. See S. Toy, *The Strongholds of India*, p. 6. It remains uncertain whether the term *hasti-parigha* has this meaning.

[104] In Divy. 220,22 the *saṃkramaṇakā* is described as being high (*ūrdhvī*): *ūrdhvī ekā nibaddhā saṃkramaṇakā*. This can be explained perhaps by the fact that the door stood higher than the base of the wall. Thus the access way above the trenches stood above the water level in them. According to Rām. 6,3,16-18, the *saṃkramāḥ* are fitted out with ballistic machines (*yantra*), columns (*stambha*), and fences (*vedikā*). In Pāli texts *esikā* are characterized as columns (*thamba*) that should be set into the earth in front of the gates. See Jāt. VI,276: *esikā ti nagara-dvāresu uṭṭhāpite esika-tthambhe*; Jāt. II,95: *nagara-dvāre nikhātā esika-tthambhā*. This corresponds to the Sanskrit *iṣika* (Mv. I,196,1; III,228,12; MPS. 34,4 (which the text edition incorrectly emends to *iṣ(ṭi)kā*). The posts, which Wheeler documented in the defensive trenches at Charsada (above, note 34), are perhaps identical with the *iṣika* mentioned in Buddhist texts. These the Kauṭilīya does not mention, nor does it talk about the freestanding gate arches (*toraṇa*) across the moat at the outer end of the way, as these purely decorative elements are beyond the horizon of the Arthaśāstra.

is characterized by 'elephant nails' (*hasti-nakha*).[105] It must be built, on the one hand (*vā*),[106] in a way that it is not subject to destruction (*asaṃhārya*)[107] by the waters of the moat. But on the other (*vā*), in places where there is no water (*nirudake*), it should be made of earth (*bhūmi-maya*). This difficult text passage finds its explanation in the manner in which the way to the city gate was laid out in Kauśāmbī. Here, the moat narrowed near the entrance gate from 144 m to 20 m. Two post-holes suggest that there was a bridge over it.[108] Here the water flowed further to the east and narrowed by means of a dam. A tamped gravel[109] road that was flanked by bastions runs through other moats, which could be flooded during sieges.

[105] This term occurs in Śisupālavadha III,68, where the city exit is described: *śanair anīyanta rayāt patanto rathāḥ kṣitiṃ hastinakhād akhedaiḥ sayatna-sūtāyata-raśmi-bhugna-grīvāgra-saṃsakta-yugais turaṃgaih.* Hultsch, transl. Leipzig 1929: "The speeding wagons would be slowly drawn from the glacis to the ground level by spirited steeds, which bore the yoke on their necks, which swayed beneath the tensed reins of careful wagoneers." Even here it is evident that the access into the gate is higher than ground level (*kṣiti*). Amarakośa 2,2,17 explains *hastinakha* as earth piled before the city gate: *kūṭam pūr-dvāri yaddhastinakhas tasmin*; see the commentary (Maheśvara): *pūr-dvāri nagara-dvāre sukhenâvatāranārtham 'krama-nimyam' yan mṛtkūṭaṃ kriyate tatra hastinakha ity ekam.* The meaning of elephant nails is unclear in Cullavagga VI,14,1a (p. 169), where a palace is mentioned with a terrace: *tena kho pana samayena Visākhā Migāramātā samghassa atthāya sālindam pāsādaṃ kārāpetu-kāmā hoti hattinakhakam.* Perhaps even here only the access way is meant, which is accessible from the terraces. Coomaraswamy EA II, p. 221 note 6 gave another interpretation: "elephant's nail [was] originally a kind of capital composed of addorsed elephants, their forefeet projecting beyond the abacus so as to make the toe-nails conspicuous when seen from below; secondly, a balcony or bridge supported by such a capital; finally, even a causeway substituted for such a bridge." See also Coomaraswamy's discussion on this in JAOS 48, p. 258f. Kangle suggests another attractive theory: "*hastinakha* is the name of the passage, so-called perhaps because it resembled a nail of the vapra appearing like an elephant's foot".

[106] In G M: *hastinakhaḥ saṃkramo 'samhāryo vā.*

[107] Cf. Kangle: "Cb Ca render *asamharya* as 'firm, made of wood' (Gaṇapati: *asamhāryaḥ sthiro dārvādi-maya ity arthaḥ*"). Kangle himself reads *saṃkramaḥ saṃhāryo* and explains *saṃhāryo* as a drawbridge, as does Meyer (translated): "The bridge (*saṃkrama*) is connecting this 'elephant's claw' with the gate and is for water forts a kind of drawbridge. Read *saṃkramaḥ saṃhāryo.*"

[108] Sharma, *The Excavations at Kauśāmbī*, p. 38-39: "There are two funnel-shaped pits, 6 ft. 2 ins. deep and 8 ft. wide at the top.... From their situation and alignment they appear to have held posts that supported an over-bridge across the channel."

[109] P. 40: "The road was made of small brickbats, gritty material, lime concretions, sherds and clay, heavily pounded." In Ujjayinī, moreover, in front of the entrance a road was revealed that had been renovated in different periods. See Ind. Arch. 1957/58, p. 34: "A thin veneer of gravel of assorted size was laid over a well-rammed and cambered soling of clay. The road of Period I was 24 ft. wide; those of Period II, varying from 23 ft. to 39 ft. in width, were marked with

31 Next, the Kauṭilīya gives the names of different kinds of gates. The first to be named is the *gopura* (gate). The context does not allows us to understand the *gopura* either as part of the gate[110] or as a designation of all gates. It can only deal with a certain gate that differs in details from on the one just described. While in the preceding description the gate was said to have a quadrangular plan, as known from Śrāvastī and other places, we might assume that *gopura* could have a plan with wide wings as one preserved at Sisupalgarh (Fig. 19). This assumption is supported by the Hathigumpha inscription, which was discovered six miles north-western of the city. In it king Khāravela reports that he repaired the *gopura*-gate, the walls, and buildings of Kaliṅganagara, which had been damaged by a storm. The equation of Sisupalgarh with the city named Kaliṅganagara in the inscription is suggested by the proximity of the inscription to Sisupalgarh, as also by the fact that restorations of the fortifications at Sisupalgarh can be demonstrated.[111] The *gopura*-gate of this inscription, therefore, can only mean the gate of Sisupalgarh.[112] A passage from the Mahābhārata illuminates the groundplan of the *gopura*-gate by comparing it with the two-winged bird Garuḍa.[113] The Kauṭilīya

cart-tracks, the gauge being 5 ft. 9 in. How the moat was crossed remained to be examined." The exterior bastion located by the road in Kauśāmbī has a counterpart in Śrāvastī (ARASI 1907/08, p. 85:): "Outside, distinct from the gate proper, there are two low mounds which apparently are the remains of outworks."

[110] As suggested by Sorabji: "The *gopura* here seems to be sort of upper turret over the gateway." Filliozat, *Gopura* 'porte de la ville', JA 1959, p. 253, also adheres to this idea: "Ici encore le *gopura* n'est pas la porte, mais la construction qui la surmounte." But the context only allows the interpretation of *gopura* as the name of an independent gatehouse. Kangle: "According to the commentators we have in this and the next as a description of different types of gates, *gopura* being the name of the gate described here."

[111] AI 5, p. 77: "During their lifetime, the structures at the gateway were repaired on several occasions. At one place on the outer side of the southern flank was observed a subsidiary wall built just to support the falling arm. The most notable fall, however, was that of the western face of the shorter arm on the south. The destruction over here seems to have been a sudden and violent one. The entire face collapsed and, to hold the rest of the structure up, an emergency aid was rushed to the spot. Bricks and brickbats were piled up against it in all sorts of ways, and it was only at a later stage that regular stone facing was provided. That these parts of India are subject to occasional cyclones is well-known, and it is not unlikely that such an occurrence may have been responsible for this large-scale destruction. " See also ibid., p. 66.

[112] JBORS 1917, p. 454: *padhame vase vāta-vihata-gopura-pākāra-nivesanaṃ paṭisaṃkhārayati.*

[113] Mbh. I,199,31: "*divipakṣagaruḍa-prakhyair dvārair ghora-pradarṣanaih guptam abhracaya-prakhair gopurair mandaropamaiḥ.*" The wording of the text, however, also permits that the comparison refers to the two door wings of the gate.

itself characterizes the *gopura* as a gate of the same height as the
wall (*prākārasamaṃ*), the third part of which resembles the snout
of a lizard (*tribhaga-godhāmukha*). The lizard's mouth is a meta-
phor for large size.[114] In the Mahāvastu, the lizard mouth refers
to an indeterminable part of the gate (*toraṇa*).[115] Perhaps the
broad wings of the Sisupalgarh gate (and presumably other, not
yet excavated gates) were regarded as resembling somehow the 32
open long mouth of a lizard.[116]

Next to be mentioned is the pond-gate (*puṣkariṇī-dvara*). It was constructed by excavating a trench (*vāpī*)[117] between the two brick rows of the wall (*prākāra-madhye*). The princess-house gate (*kumārī-pura*)[118] is laid out in the form of an atrium house (*catuḥśāla*)[119] with 1 ½ times the space (*adhyārdhāntaraṃ*) and with [shooting] holes (? *sāṇikam*). Finally, the long wooden gate (? *muṇḍaka-dvāra*)[120] is two-storied (*dvi-tala*) with an upper floor consisting of beams (? *muṇḍa-harmya*). The chapter closes with the statement that building directions vary according to the

[114] Cf. H. Lüders: *Von indischen Tieren*, ZDMG 96, 1942, p. 25.

[115] Mv. II,193,15: *godhāmukha-niryūha-dṛdhārgalaka-pota-toraṇe*, "(in the city of Kapilavastu), the doors of which consist of lizard mouths, little towers, stout bolts and pigeon friezes".

[116] Similarly, in YL 128R4 ed. p. 86, the space (*vivara*) between the large and the second toe are compared with the mouth (*mukha*) of a Makara.

[117] The term *vāpī* also occurs with the meaning "trench" also in KA. 2,5,2, where the excavation of a subterranean chamber (*bhūmigṛha*) is described. Since the space between the two encasing brick faces contained earth, a trench had to be excavated in order to break a hole for the gate in the bricks at the foot of the wall. This gate probably was named 'lotus pond gate' because the trench resembled the trench to be dug out for the construction a lotus pond. Hardly probably is Kangle's assumption that, "the *vāpī* would appear to be a sort of hollow into which the enemy soldiers would be trapped, should they happen to surge through the gate". Similarly, Meyer imagines the trench as an arsenal (translated): "Also the 'lotus pond', which has produced so much headache, is thus not filled with flowers but with the requisites for a 'hospitable reverence' toward the enemy — as the epics often call a battle —, that is, with weapons."

[118] *kumārīpura* is named in Vāyup. together with a *svastika* gate: *saudhocca-vapra-prākāraṃ sarvvataś cātakāvṛtaṃ tad ekaṃ svastika-dvāraṃ kumārīpuram eva ca.*

[119] *catuḥśāla* is a farm made of four long houses with barrel-vaulted roofs, see Figs. 24 and 25. See Vogel's comment on the house-forms in Bhita (AR 1909/10, p. 41): "As regards the general plan of the houses, they all consist of a central courtyard enclosed by a row of rooms on all four sides. Hence the Sanskrit term *catuḥśāla*, meaning a 'building of four halls (*sala*)'." Perhaps the *catuḥśāla* gate is called 'residence of the princesses' because the palaces of the princesses were typically built in a *catuḥśāla* design.

[120] Here, the meaning of *muṇḍa* is entirely uncertain. Konow, *Kauṭilīya Studies*, Oslo 1945, p. 63, expressed the supposition that the *muṇḍaka-dvāra* is a door fashioned of hewn tree trunks. Kangle translated "... a bare room with two stories, as the *mundaka* gate". Meyer (translated): "...an iron house of two stories and with an iron door".

characteristics of the land (*bhūmi*) and according to the building material (*dravya*) that is available.[121]

The archaeological research on Indian urban defenses is still in its early stages, so that it cannot solve all problems of the chapter on fortifications of the Kauṭilīya. Wherever we can confront the text with the results from excavations, they illuminate the difficult passages often in a surprisingly simple manner. Difficulties come from our insufficient knowledge of the material, not from an unclear manner of expression, nebulousness, or a lack of objectivity of the text. Just the opposite, the chapter distinguishes itself through a precision and reliability in the exposition. Certainly, one should not expect from it a systematic description of the building process or instructions for the constructor. It may be based on a construction manual, but the chapter was written for the patron, not for the builder. Therefore, it provides only those excerpts from the manual that address items relevant for the state's inspection. Those items were trend-setting in construction work. Therefore, their interpretation can also give archaeologists important hints for their excavations.

[121] The final sentence and the associated verse no longer belong in this context. According to Kangle, "s. 33 should be detached from this paragraph".

Lexicographical Results

Technical terms on fortification in Kauṭilīya Arthaśāstra 2.3, re-interpreted in light of archaeological evidence.

aṭṭālaka	rectangular wall-tower, Ch. 2, note 48; Figs. 10-14.
asaṃhārya	causeway to the city gate, indestructible [by the water of the moat], Ch. 2, note 107.
āgantutoyapūrṇa	moat, filled with water that is channeled [from the riverside], p. 60f.
āṇidvara	a side door, Ch. 2, note 102.
indrakīla	the threshold of a city gate, Ch. 2, note 101.
indrakośa	an embrasure in the city wall, Ch. 2, note 63; Figs. 14, 28.
utsedhasamāva-kṣepasopāna	wall tower with trap-stairs parallel with its vertical axis, Ch. 2, note 49.
ūrdhvacaya	vaulted rampart, Ch. 2, note 12.
aiṣṭaka	city wall built of bricks, Ch. 2, note 14; Fig. 1.
kapiśīrṣaka	a merlon of a crenellated parapet, Ch. 2, note 18; Fig. 1a.
kāṣṭhamaya	city wall made of timber, Ch. 2, notes 20-21; Fig. 3.
kumārīpura	a city gate having the plan of a princess-house (= the *catuḥśāla*-plan), Ch. 2, note 118.
kumbhakukṣika	rampart with the shape of the belly of a pot, p. 60f.; Fig. 9.
gūḍhabhittisopāna	staircase on the right side of the gate-house with a light wall that covers it, Ch. 2, notes 95-96; Fig. 19.
gopura	wing-shaped (?) gate-house, p. 80f.; Fig. 19 ?.
channapatha	hidden path outside the rampart, Ch. 2, note 70.
tālamūla	city wall with a foundation reinforced with palmyra-beams, Ch. 2, note 17.
toyāntika	moat fed by (spring)-water, Ch. 2, note 9.
tridhanuṣkādhiṣṭhāna	embrasure connected with a position for three archers, p. 71f.
tribhāgagodhāmukha	*gopura* gate one third of which is a long

	flanked gateway resembling the snout of a lizard, p. 81.
tribhāgamūla	moat with a bottom width one-third of the surface width, Ch. 2, note 3; Fig. 8.
devapatha	walk along the wall behind the embrasures, Ch. 2, note 65.
dvāra	rectangular city gate-house, p. 72f.; Figs. 20-23, 28, 30.
parikhā	moat, p. 59f.; Figs. 4, 8.
parigha	cross-bar across the door panels at the inner side of the gate-house, p. 78 note 99, note 100.
pāṣāṇeṣṭakābaddha-pārśva	moat, banks revetted with pebbles or bricks, Ch. 2, notes 99-100.
puṣkariṇīdvara	pond-gate, i.e., passage through the city-wall, the mud filling of which was removed at this place by digging a pond-like pit, p. 81f.
pṛthuśilāsaṃhita	city wall built of large rough stones, Ch. 2, note 19; Fig. 2.
pratolī	postern gate – a rectangular turret with an upper story, Ch. 2, note 60; Fig. 15.
pradakṣiṇasopāna	staircase on the left side of the gate-house with a right-hand turn, p. 77; Fig. 19.
prākāra	city wall, p. 61f.; Figs. 1-7.
bhūmimaya	causeway to the city gate, made of earth, p. 79f.
maṇḍalaka	inwardly curved city wall at the gate-house, p. 74f.; Figs. 20, 30.
muṇḍakadvāra	beam-gate with an upper story consisting of beams, p. 81.
rathacaryasamcara	city wall with an ascent for war chariots, Ch. 2, note 16.
vapra	rampart, p. 60f.; Figs. 4-9.
viṣkambhacaturaśra	wall-tower rectangular in plan, Ch. 2, note 49.
śaila	city wall of undressed stone, Ch. 2, note 19; Fig. 2.
saṃkrama	causeway to the city gate, p. 78.
saharmyadvitala	two-story postern gate, p. 71; Fig. 15.

sāpidhānacchidra-phalakasahita	embrasure with a loop-holed wooden shutter, Ch. 2, note 64, Fig. 14(?).
sīmāgṛha	border room on the right side of the gate-house, p. 76f.; Figs. 19, 22.
hastiparigha	bar across the door leaves on the outer side of the gate-house, reinforcement against the assault of elephants (?), Ch. 2, note 103.

The drawings are based on the following publications:

Fig. 1. Marshall/Foucher, *The Monuments of Sanchi,* II, pl. XXXV, XV, XL.
Fig. 2. AI 4, pl. XXV.
Fig. 3. AI 4, p. 99.
Fig. 4. After KA. 2,3,4-7.
Fig. 5. Ind. Arch. 1961/62, p. 6.
Fig. 6. Krishna Deva/Mishra Vijayakanta, *Vaiśālī Excavations* 1950, Fig. 6 (cf. Fig. 3).
Fig. 7. AI 5, p. 73.
Fig. 8. Ind. Arch. 1956/57, p. 22.
Fig. 9. G.R. Sharma, *The Excavations at Kauśāmbī,* Fig. 3.
Fig. 10. ARASI 1911/12, p. 29.
Fig. 11. AI 4, p. 93.
Fig. 12. AI 4, pl. XXII.
Fig. 13. Marshall/Foucher, *The Monuments of Sanchi,* II, pl. XV.
Fig. 14. Ingholt, *Gandharan Art in Pakistan,* p. 464.
Fig. 15. Marshall/Foucher, *The Monuments of Sanchi,* II, pl. XV.
Fig. 16. Marshall/Foucher, *The Monuments of Sanchi,* II, pl. XV.
Fig. 17. *Arch. Survey of Southern India,* Vol. I, pl. XXVII.
Fig. 18. After Fig. 16 and Fig. 17.
Fig. 19. P. Yule, *Early Historic Sites in Orissa,* Delhi 2006, Fig. 28.
Fig. 20. ARASI 1907/08, pl. XXXI.
Fig. 21. Ind. Arch. 1957/58, p. 7.
Fig. 22. Marshall, *Taxila,* III, pl. X, cf. AI 4, pl. XXII.
Fig. 23. ARASI 1911/12, p. 29 (graphic reconstruction).
Fig. 24. W. Judeich, *Topographie von Athen* (Handbuch d. Altertumswissenschaften III. 2.2, p. 137).
Fig. 25. *The Excavations at Dura-Europos* I, pl. I, cf. II, p. 6ff.).
Fig. 26. C. W. Blegen *et al.*, *Troy* I, p. 2, 417.
Fig. 27. ABIA 16, pl. XLII.
Fig. 28. Ingholt, *Gandharan Art in Pakistan,* p. 152.
Fig. 29. Ph. Vogel, *La sculpture de Mathurā,* pl. XXIIIa.
Fig. 30. After KA. 2,3,16.

I. Fortification walls

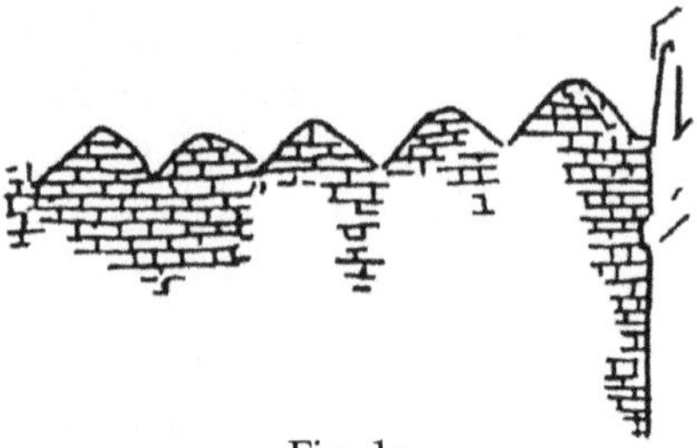

Fig. 1a

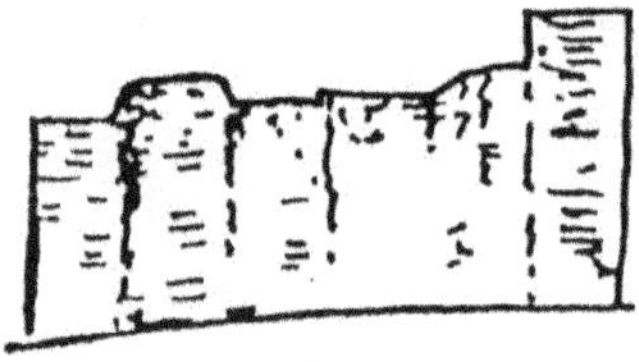

Fig. 1b

Fig. 1c

Fig. 1 Representations in Sanci

Fig. 2 Natural stone wall in Old Rājagṛha

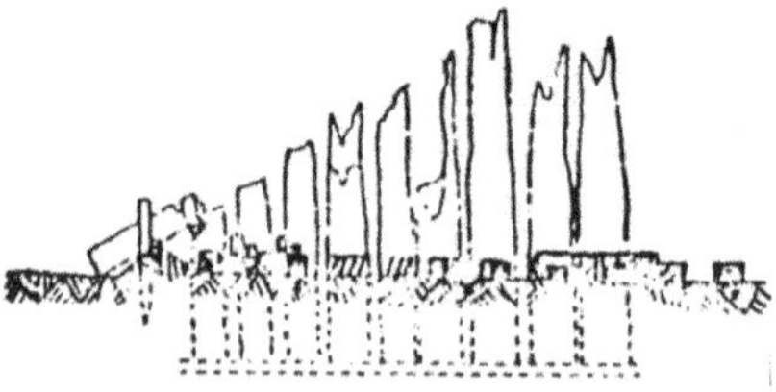

Fig. 3 Palisades in Pāṭaliputra

II. Sections of fortifications

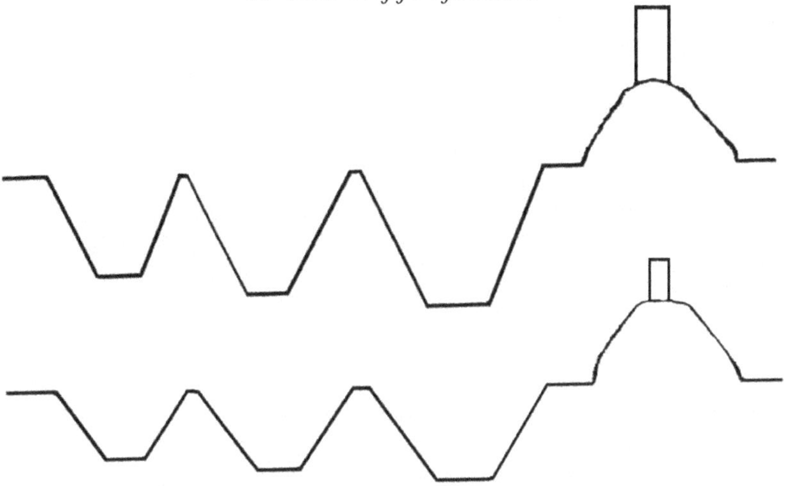

Fig. 4 Section as prescribed (max./min.) in the Kauṭilīya Arthaśāstra

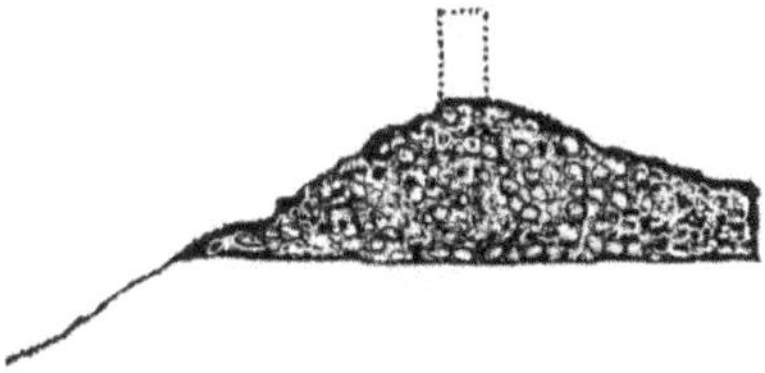

Fig. 5 New Rājagṛha

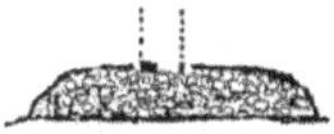

Fig. 6 Vaiśālī

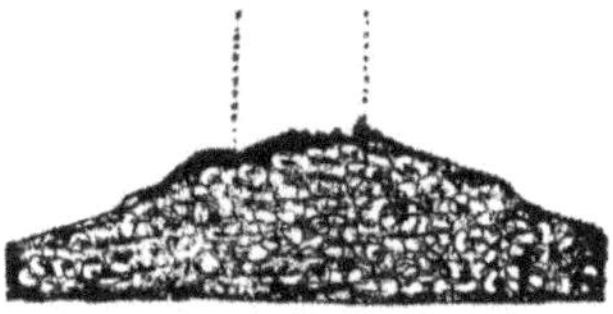

Fig. 7 Sisupalgarh

Fig. 8 Ujjayinī

Fig. 9 Kauśāmbī

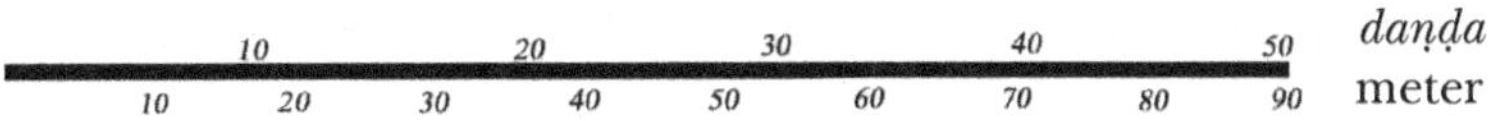

III. Towers

Fig. 10 Bhita

Fig. 11 Old Rājagṛha

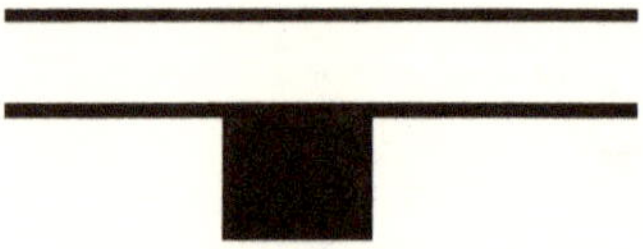

Fig. 12 Taxila (Sirkap)

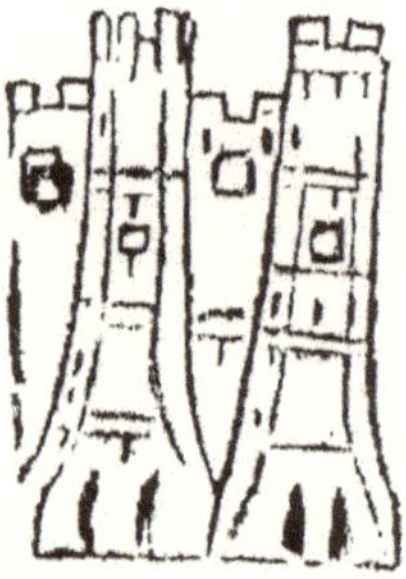

Fig. 14 Representation in Gandhara

Fig. 13 Representation in Sanci

Fig. 15 Representation of a postern gate in Sanci

IV. City gates

Fig. 16 Representation in Sanci

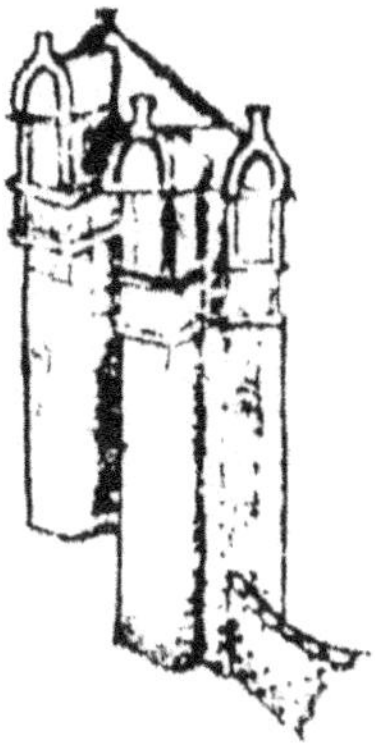

Fig. 17 Representation in Amaravati

Fig. 18 Plan according to the representations

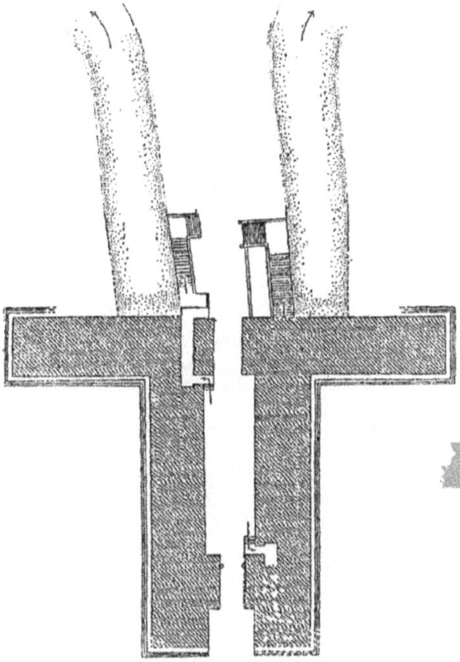

Fig. 19 Śiśupālgarh, western gate

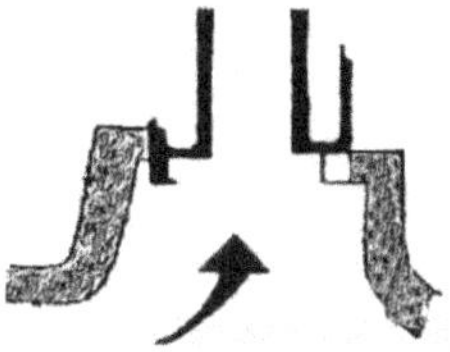

Fig. 20 Srāvastī, Nausahra gate

Fig. 21 Nagarjunikonda, western gate

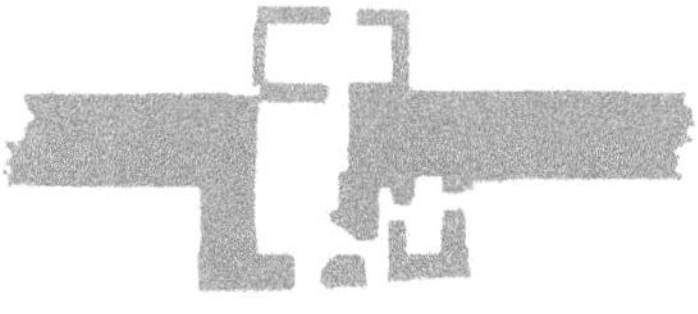

Fig. 22 Taxila (Sirkap), northern gate

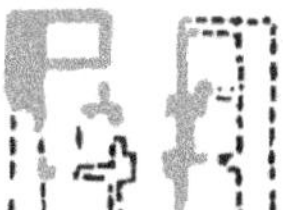

Fig. 23 Bhita, gate

Fig. 24 Athens, Dipylon

Fig. 25 Dura-Europos, Palmyra gate

Fig. 26 Troy 6, eastern gate

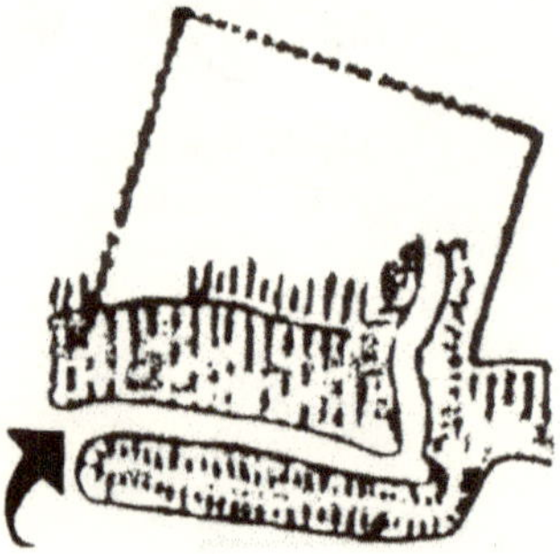

Fig. 27 Kauśāmbī, scheme of the eastern gate (diminished)

Fig. 28 Representation in Gandhara

Fig. 29 Representation in Mathurā

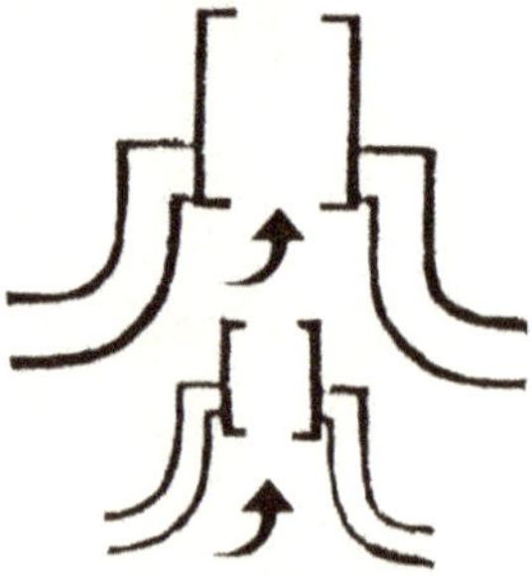

Fig. 30 Plan as prescribed (max./min.) in the Kauṭilīya Arthaśāstra

Chapter 3

The Model of the City in Narrative Ajanta Paintings[*]

In order to visualize the structure of an old Indian city we are still almost completely dependent on random mentions in contemporary literature. Representations in reliefs generally do not depict cities but rather individual buildings. Moreover, excavations reveal building plans of houses, but not of urban structures. The narrative paintings of Ajanta complement the available source material in a welcome manner. Since the large-area paintings recently became completely available as line drawings,[1] it is possible to gain an insight into their formal structure. It becomes evident that the painters by no means spread the depicted scenes over the surface in a random fashion but rather imbedded them into an ideal plan of the city. Although the requirements of the narrative, as well as the size and shape of the available pictorial wall, necessitated many variations, the paintings, divested of the figures acting in them, reveal a generalized sketch of the cityscape.

Due to the narrative content, in nearly all the paintings the royal palace occupies the foreground. It was also the most prominent building structure. It was not only the residence of the king and his court. and seat of the state administration, it also served as the military, economic, and cultural center of the city. Thus this palace did not consist of simply a single building; it was rather a complex of halls that were grouped around several interior

[*] Translated from the German "Das Schema der Stadt in narrativen Ajantamalereien", in: *Vanamālā, Festschrift für Adelbert J. Gail*, Berlin 2006, p. 214-18.

[1] D. Schlingloff, *Erzählende Wandmalereien/ Narrative Wall Paintings, Vol. I Interpretation; Vol. II Supplement; Vol. III Plates* (*Ajanta - Handbuch der Malereien / Handbook of the Paintings 1*), Wiesbaden 2000; idem, *Guide to the Ajanta Paintings, Vol. I, Narrative Wall Paintings*, New Delhi 1999.

courts containing smaller buildings, for example, court tents (Fig. 8), court pavilions (Figs. 1, 8), or circular halls (Fig. 6). The function of the different buildings can be read from the events depicted. There were council and audience halls (Figs. 1, 2, 6, 7), schoolrooms (Figs. 1, 6), kitchens (Fig. 1), dining halls (Fig. 1), workshops (Fig. 8), and elephant and horse stables (Figs. 1, 4, 6), as well as sport halls (Fig. 1) and sport arenas (Fig. 6), which might have been located outside of the palace proper. The quarters of the king and queen, as well as those of the crown prince, were separate (Fig. 5). The only building that is depicted with two (Figs. 4, 7) or three (Fig. 2) stories may be the *antaḥpura,* the house of the king and his female court. In addition to the gates to the entire palace complex (Figs. 1-8), this 'inner building' had a separate gate (Figs. 2, 4) and a wall (Fig. 2). The main gate of the palace complex (Fig. 2) leads to the main avenue of the city, which was flanked by shops, behind which the upper stories of dwellings are visible (Figs. 1-5). Separate houses of citizens (Figs. 2, 4) and a city hall (Fig. 3) appear only when the narrative requires them. Representations of city gates (Figs. 1-7) cannot be distinguished from those of the palace gates; the city rampart and moat are not depicted.

Thus the cityscape of the paintings corresponds to an ideal image of the old Indian city known from the contemporary narrative literature and from the handbooks of statecraft. The interpretation of architectural details requires some care. The city gates require special attention since the basic requirements of fortifications and excavation results show that the city gates were never simple portals, as the palace gates were (see Ch. 2). Reacting to the pressure of compositional limits, the painters copied the cliché of the palace gate in depicting the city gate. Even with regard to the representation of buildings not all of the details correspond to reality. The necessity to visualize every event of the story depicted certainly lead to representations depicted in open column halls of events that in reality occurred behind closed walls. An exact picture of old Indian secular buildings, therefore, will only be possible when further excavation results become available.

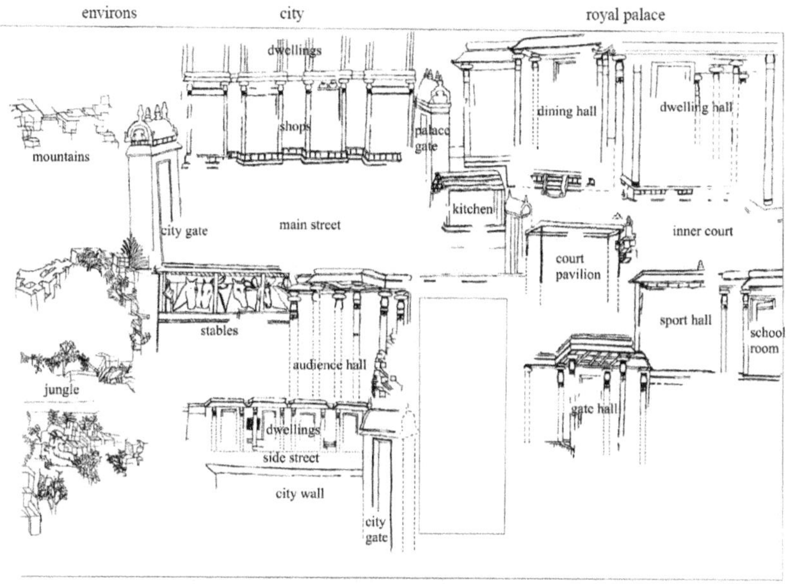

Fig. 1 Sutasoma (No. 57/XVII, 52)

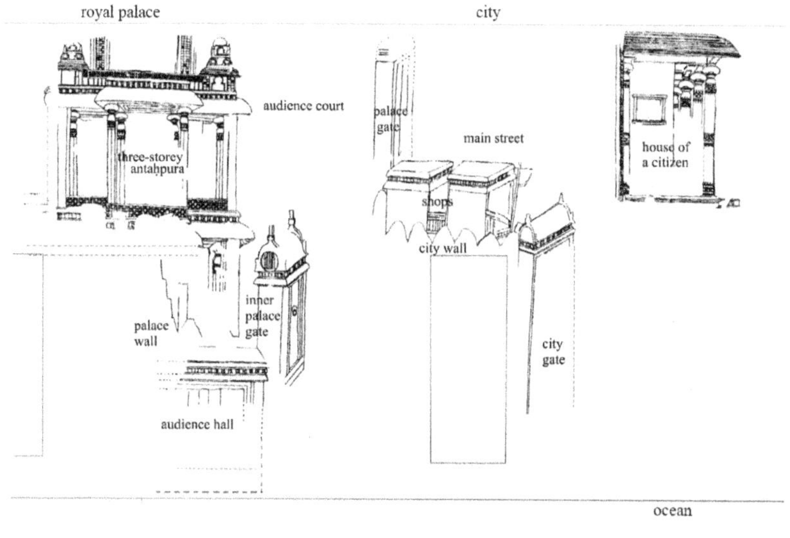

Fig. 2 Siṃhala (No. 58/XVII, 57)

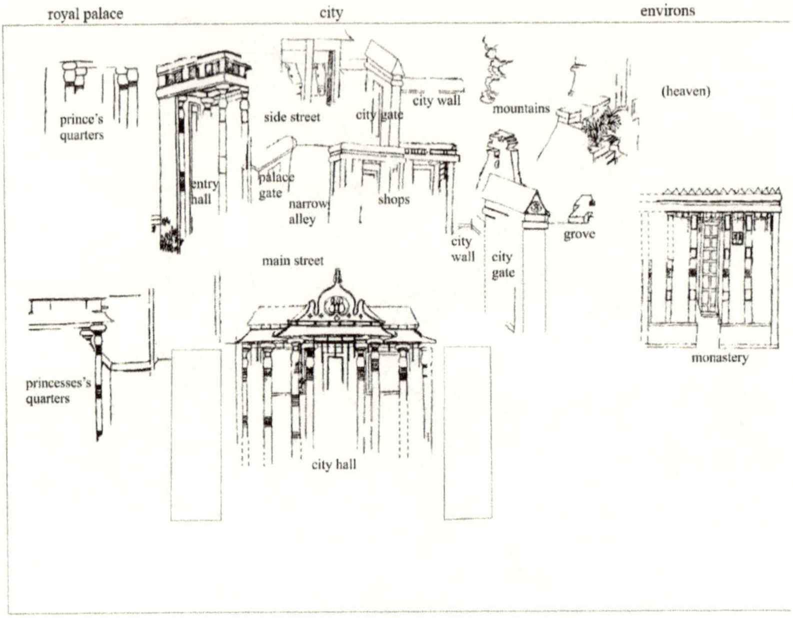

Fig. 3 Nanda (No. 73/XVI, 34)

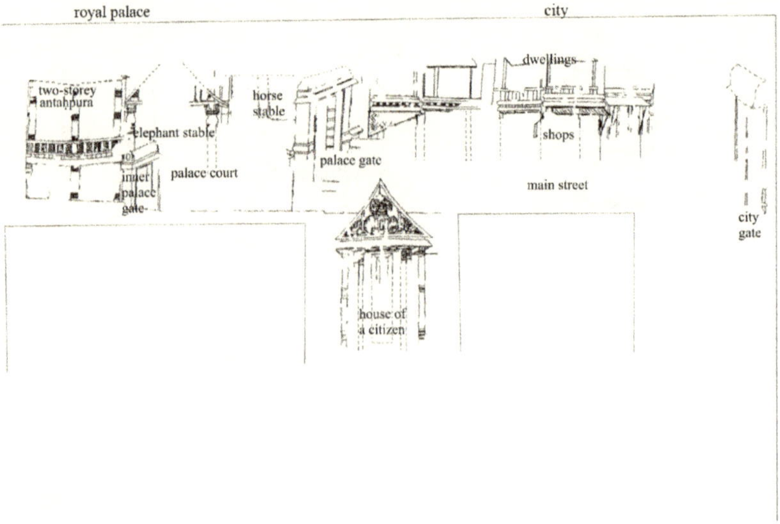

Fig. 4 Dhanapāla (No. 77/XVII, 41)

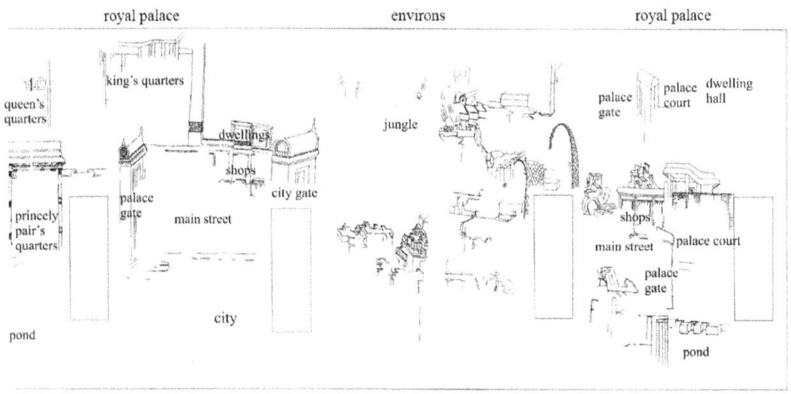

Fig. 5 Viśvantara (No. 43/XVI, 49f.)

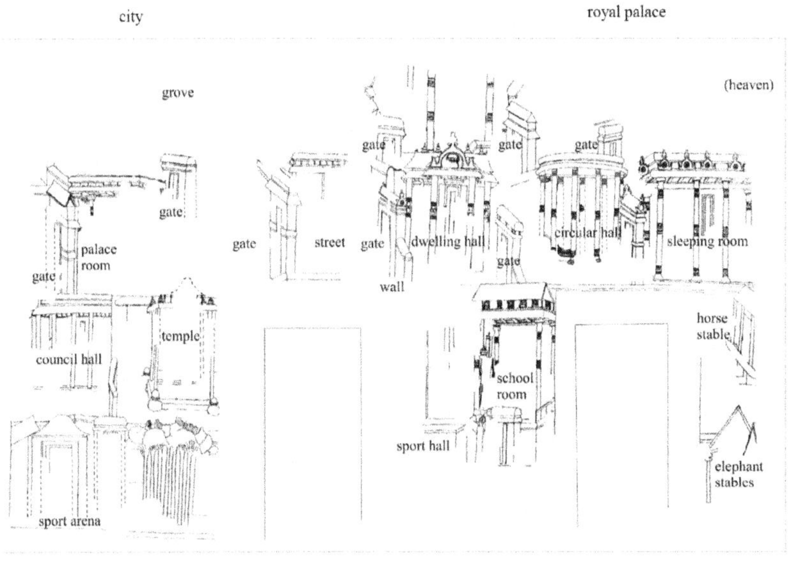

Fig. 6 Bhagavan (No. 64/XVI, 37f.)

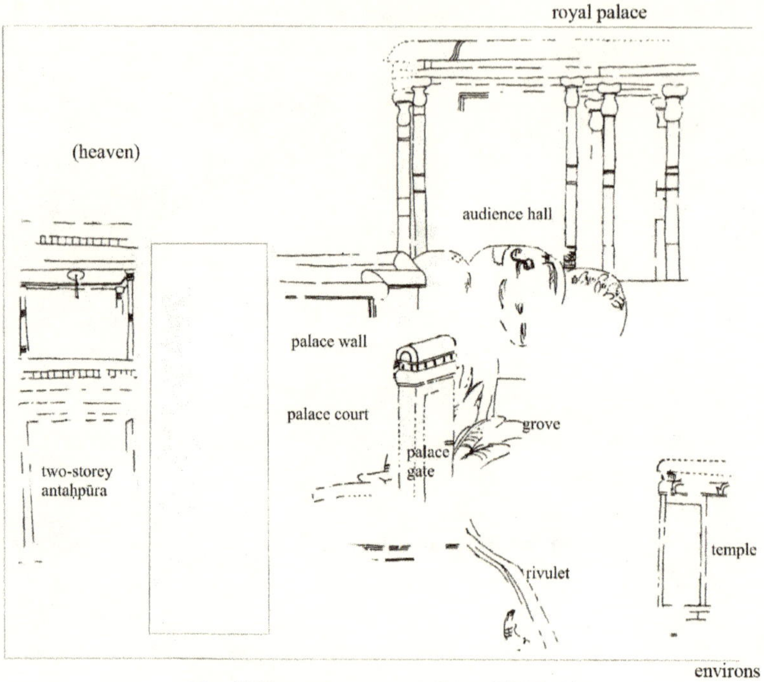

Fig. 7 Bhagavatprasuti (No. 65/II, 17)

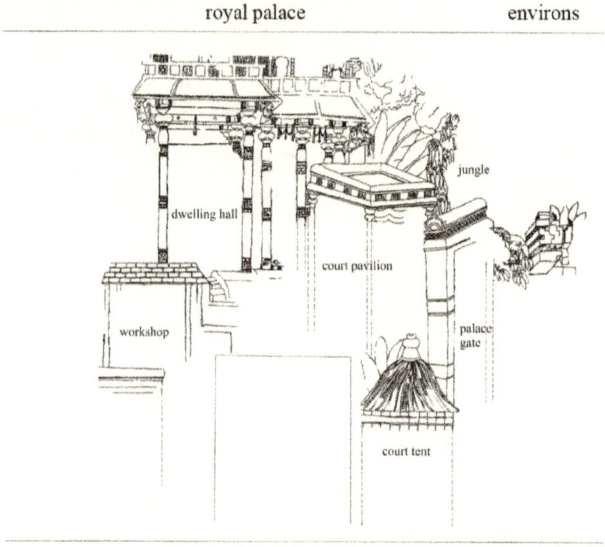

Fig. 8 Janaka (No. 45/I, 5)

List of Abbreviations

ABIA	*Annual Bibliography of Indian Archaeology*, Leiden.
ABORI	*Annals of the Bhandarkar Oriental Research Institute*, Poona.
AI	*Ancient India, Bulletin of the Archaeological Survey of India*, New Delhi.
Altekar	A.S, Altekar/V. Misra, *Report on Kumrahar Excavations 1951-55*, Patna 1959.
Ap.	*Apadāna*, ed. M.Z. Lilley, London, Pāli Text Society 1925-27.
ARASI	*Annual Report of the Archaeological Survey of India*, 1902/03-1936/37, Calcutta.
Arch. Or.	*Archiv Orientalni, Journal of the Oriental Institute of the Czechoslovak Academy of Sciences*, Prague.
Art. As.	*Artibus Asiae, The Quarterly of Asiatic Art, Archaeology and all fields of Asiatic Science*, New York.
ASIR	*Archaeological Survey of India*, Reports (by A. Cunningham, *et al.*), Vols. 1-23, Simla.
Avim.	*The Avimāraka of Bhāsa*, ed. T. Gaṇapati Śāstrī, Trivandrum Sanskrit Series XX, 1912.
Beal	*Si-yu-ki, Buddhist Records of the Western World, translated from the Chinese of Hiuen Tsiang (A.D. 629)*, by S. Beal, Vols. I, II, London 1906.
Bharhut	A. Cunningham, *The Stūpa of Bharhut*, (repr.) Varanasi 1962.
BHSD	*Buddhist Hybrid Sanskrit Dictionary*, by F. Edgerton, New Haven 1953.
BV	*Bhāratīya Vidyā, A Quarterly Research Organ of the Bhāratīya Vidyā Bhavan*, Bombay.

Cār.	*Cārudatta*, in *Bhāsanāṭakacakram*, ed. C.R. Devadhar, Poona 1962.
CPD	*A Critical Pali Dictionary*, ed. V. Trenckner (*et al.*), Copenhagen 1924ff.
D.	*The Dīgha Nikāya*, ed. T.W. Rhys Davids/J.E. Carpenter, London, Pāli Text Society (repr.) 1966.
Divy.	*Divyāvadāna*, ed. Cowell/Neil, Cambridge 1886.
Daś.	*Daṇḍin, Daśakumāracarita*, ed. N.B. Godabole/ K.P. Parab, Bombay ³1898.
EA	*Eastern Art*, Philadelphia.
GRI	*Geographical Review of India*, Calcutta.
Harṣac.	*Bāṇa, Harṣacarita*, ed. K.P. Parab, Bombay ²1897.
IIJ	*Indo-Iranian Journal*, Leiden.
Ind. Ant.	*The Indian Antiquary*, Bombay.
Ind. Arch.	*Indian Archaeology, A Review*, New Delhi.
JAHRS	*Journal of the Andhra Historical Research Society*, Rajahmundry.
JAOS	*Journal of the American Oriental Society*, Baltimore (*et al.*).
JBORS	*Journal of the Bihar (and Orissa) Research Society*, Patna.
JASB	*Journal of the Asiatic Society of Bengal*, Calcutta.
Jāt.	*The Jātaka*, ed. by V. Fausboll, Vols. I-VII, (repr.) London 1962.
JBBRAS	*Journal of the Bombay Branch of the Royal Asiatic Society*, Bombay.
JESHO	*Journal of the Economic and Social History of the Orient*, Leiden.
JM	*Āryaśūra, Jātakamālā*, ed. H. Kern Boston 1891.
JOIB	*Journal of the Oriental Institute*, Baroda.
JRAS	*Journal of the Royal Asiatic Society of Great Britain and Ireland*, London.
KA.	R.P. Kangle, *The Kauṭilīya Artaśāstra, Part I, A Critical Edition with a Glossary, Part II, an English translation*, Part 3, A Study Bombay 1960-65.
Kād.	*Bāṇa, Kādambarī*, ed. P. Peterson Bombay ²1889.
Kāmas.	*Vātsyāyana, Kāmasūtra*, ed. Devadutta Sastri, Varanasi 1964.
Kathās.	*The Kathāsaritsāgara of Somadeva*, ed. P. Durgaprāsad and K.P. Parab, Bombay 1889.
Kum.	*Kālidāsa, Kumārasaṃbhava*, ed, M.A. Karandikar, Bombay 1950.

M.	*The Majjima Nikāya*, ed. V. Trenckner, London, Pāli Text Society, (repr.) 1964.
Mahābhāṣya	*The Vyākaraṇa-Mahābhāshya of Patañjali*, ed. F. Kielhorn, Vols. I, II, Bombay 1892-1906.
Manu	*The Manava Dharma Sastra*, ed. V.N. Mandlik, Bombay 1886.
MASI	*Memoirs of the Archaeological Survey of India*, Calcutta.
Mbh.	*The Mahābhārata, for the first time critically edited* by V.S. Sukthankar (*et al.*) Poona 1933ff.
Meyer	J.J. Meyer, *Das altindische Buch vom Welt- und Staatsleben, das Arthasastra des Kautilya*, Leipzig 1926.
Mil.	*Milindapañha*, ed. V. Trenckner, London 1880.
MPS	*Das Mahāparinirvāṇasūtra, Text in Sanskrit und Tibetisch, verglichen mit dem Pāli nebst einer Übersetzung der chinesischen Entsprechung im Vinaya der Mūlasarvāstivādins*, ed. E. Waldschmidt, Parts II, III, Berlin 1951.
MR	*The Modern Review*, Calcutta.
Mṛcch.	*Śūdraka, Mṛcchakaṭika*, ed. N.B. Godabole, Bombay 1896.
Mudr.	*Viśākhadatta, Mudrārākṣasa*, ed. A. Hillebrandt, Breslau 1912.
Mv	*Mahāvastu*, publ. E. Sénart, Paris 1882-97.
NAGW	*Nachrichten von der Gesellschaft der Wissenschaften in Göttingen, Phil.-hist. Klasse.*
P	Pāli.
Pādat.	*The Pādatāḍitaka of Śyāmilaka, A text-critical Edition*, by G.H. Schokker, Part I, The Hague 1966.
Patil	*The Antiquarian Remains in Bihar*, by B.R. Patil, Patna 1963.
PTSD	*The Pali Text Society's Pali-English Dictionary*, ed. T.W. Rhys Davids/W. Stede, London.
PW	*Sanskrit-Wörterbuch* by O. Böhtlingk and R. Roth, I-VII, St. Petersburg 1855ff.
Rām.	*The Vālmīki-Rāmāyaṇa, Critically edited for the first time*, Vols. Iff. Baroda 1960ff.
SBE	*The Sacred Books of the East*, Oxford.
Stein	*Megasthenes und Kauṭilya*, by O. Stein, Vienna 1921.
Vas.	*Vasiṣṭhasmṛti*, in *Smṛtīnāṃ Samuccayaḥ*, Ānandāśramasaṃskṛtagranthāvaliḥ, Granthāṅga 48, Khristābdāḥ 1929
Vayup	*The Vayumahapuranam*, ed. K.S. Das, Bombay.
Waddell	L.A. Waddell, *Report on Excavations at Pāṭaliputra*, Calcutta 1903.

WZKSO	*Wiener Zeitschrift für die Kunde Süd- und Ostasiens*, Vienna.
YL	*Ein buddhistisches Yogalehrbuch*, ed. D. Schlingloff, Berlin, 1964, repr. Munich 2006.
ZDMG	*Zeitschrift der Deutschen Morgenländischen Gesellschaft*, Leipzig-Wiesbaden.

Index

About the Author

Dieter Schlingloff, Honorary Professor, University of Leipzig, former Head of the Department of Indology and Iranian Studies at the University of Munich, Germany, began his academic career 60 years ago with studies on the Berlin collection of Buddhist Sanskrit manuscripts from Central Asia. Among other projects, he edited collections of Buddhist hymns (*Buddhistische Stotras,* Berlin 1955), texts on Sanskrit metrics (*Chandoviciti,* Berlin 1958), lists of doctrinal terms (*Daśottara-sūtra* IX-X, Berlin 1962), and primarily, a treatise on Buddhist Yoga which describes the visions of a meditating monk (*Ein buddhistisches Yogalehrbuch,* I, Berlin 1964, II, Berlin 1966; enlarged and revised edition 2006). The author then turned his attention to aspects of ancient Indian culture, especially the development of towns and cities, which culminated in the present study. His more recent studies have been devoted to Buddhist art, in particular to the Ajanta paintings. The results of these investigations were published in the *Studies in the Ajanta Paintings,* Delhi 1988, and in a comprehensive *Ajanta Handbook of the Paintings,* Vol. I, Wiesbaden 2000 (Indian edition in preparation), in combination with a *Guide to the Ajanta Paintings,* Delhi 1999.

www.ingramcontent.com/pod-product-compliance
Lightning Source LLC
Chambersburg PA
CBHW020006290326
41935CB00007B/324
* 9 7 8 1 7 8 3 0 8 3 4 9 7 *